Dogs Against Crime

DOX

Dogs Against Crime

True Accounts of Canine

Training and Exploits in

Worldwide Police Work

Past and Present

by Albert Orbaan

ILLUSTRATED WITH PHOTOGRAPHS AND
WITH DRAWINGS BY THE AUTHOR

THE JOHN DAY COMPANY   NEW YORK

The John Day Company
257 Park Avenue South
New York, N.Y. 10010

an **Intext** publisher

Published on the same day in Canada by
Longmans Canada Limited.

Library of Congress Catalogue Card Number: 68-11294

PRINTED IN THE UNITED STATES OF AMERICA

Acknowledgments

THE AUTHOR is extremely grateful to Police Chief Edward Dixon, Patrolman Gary Steinberg and other members of the Freeport, Long Island, police for permitting him to witness police dog training exercises and providing him with valuable information on their K-9 operations.

Warmest thanks are also extended to the following people and organizations for providing essential information:

Adam "Scotty" Denholm, formerly of the Sydney, N.S.W., Australia, police, for information on the Windsor murder case; Mrs. Kathleen Zammarano and Giovanni Maimone, formerly of the Rome police, for detailed data on the exploits of Dox; London Metropolitan Police for extensive textual material regarding the London dog division; Wilfred Funk and George G. Harrap publishing companies for permission to use material from the book *My Dog Rex* by Arthur Holman; Chief Superintendent Nielsen Ouro of the Copenhagen, Denmark, police for a detailed account of Danish police dog operations; members of the American Kennel Club in New York City for providing special information and the use of its extensive library for research; Hutchinson Publishing Company of London for permission to adapt material from the book *My Forty Years with Dogs* by Edwin Richardson.

The Fidelco Breeders' Foundation of Bloomfield, Connecticut;

8 ACKNOWLEDGMENTS

Inter-Nationes of Bonn, Germany; the K-9 division of the Baltimore, Maryland, police; and the publicity and security departments of Macy's department store in New York City were likewise very helpful in furnishing the author with photographic and textual material.

Contents

Prologue, 13

1. The Furred Lightning, 15

2. Dog of Epirus, 40

3. The Hunters and the Hunted, 48

4. The Adventures of Edwin Richardson, 68

5. The K-9 Trailblazers, 95

6. "Il Gigante," 114

7. Sleuth of London, 152

8. Brandy 4, Nero, Christel and
   Some Others, 187

9. Terror at Christmas, 203

In Conclusion, 221

Bibliography, 229

Index, 233

Dogs Against Crime

Prologue

IN earth's dim past—possibly 100,000 years ago—the two-legged being and one of the four-footed animals became friends. It has been this animal's destiny since then to obey, guard and serve mankind in varying fashions in daylight and darkness.

When this bond first came about, the animal may have been huge or very small, furry or sleek-hided. It probably was dissimilar to its kin on earth today. How, when and where this alliance between man and this creature started will be a mystery forever. What we do know is that the animal was a dog.

In the sweep of centuries more and more of these creatures have befriended man, assuming many shapes and varied colors, tasting in full measure both cruelty and kindness, joy and despair. The fealty born in time's lost moment has endured in peace and war and will prevail as long as dogs exist.

The one absolutely unselfish friend a man may have in this selfish world . . . is the dog.—From the notable speech made by Graham Vest at a trial in Missouri in 1870 involving the killing of a foxhound named Drum

1

The Furred Lightning

THE blond young man in the blue jeans and pullover suddenly raised his right arm, crooked it slightly and fired point-blank at the unleashed dog crouched on the ground about ten paces in front of him.

He loosed two shots in quick succession but there was no

third. The mere shift in his arm position, before he had even pulled the trigger the first time, had prompted counteraction so fast that the human eye could scarcely follow it.

Obeying a muttered command from another man standing next to him in the open field, the dog, a German shepherd, heaved and bounded toward his opponent. No human could match the speed of this takeoff. Fangs bared, totally uncowed by the revolver barrel or the two shots, the dog twisted upward slightly and clamped his teeth in the sleeve covering the man's right forearm.

Without relaxing his grip, the brown and black dog fell back on all fours, throwing his foe off balance. Threshing and pulling, the animal swung his opponent first in one direction and then in another, at one moment almost causing him to stumble and fall.

The revolver slipped from the man's grasp as he sought vainly to shake off 100 pounds of fighting, snarling fury clamped to his arm. In seconds his combat potentialities were virtually nullified, his movements resembling those of a drunk executing a confused dance in the bright October sun.

This tug-of-war, which could have continued for some time before a decision was reached, terminated almost as rapidly as it had begun. The man who had uttered the first order—which was "Get him"—shouted another command, "Break." Responding instantly, the dog released his grip, shook his head, gave a low growl and quietly trotted back and sat down next to the man giving the orders.

Heeding a command to "sit," he then received a friendly pat on the head and the accolade "Good dog." Tail wagging, the dog, a magnificent specimen, looked upward toward the man in a manner which clearly showed that the animal fully appreciated the dual compliment. It was justified. One of the most difficult maneuvers in this dog's specialized training had been executed without one slip on the animal's part.

No one was hurt or really frightened by this encounter which took place in the town of Freeport, Long Island, about forty minutes by commuter train from New York City. The two men were policemen, Patrolman George Nicolino, the "gunman," and Patrolman Gary Steinberg, one of this country's outstanding police dog trainers.

The only nervous person around was myself, in spite of the reassuring presence nearby of George, Gary and another patrolman, John McGoldrick, all in pullovers, jeans and sneakers. Although the onlooker may know there is no particular danger involved, the mere sight of a police dog on the offensive instills a desire to be somewhere else, way up a tree or behind a solid door.

The whole operation was routine, part of the weekly training, or refresher program, of the K-9 division of the Freeport police. At that time—1965—Freeport was the only place in New York State where the local police had formally enrolled and trained these formidable four-footed cops. Since then police of Suffolk County have instituted a K-9 unit with dogs trained by police at Freeport, which is in Nassau county. All the highly trained dogs are German shepherds, also widely referred to as Alsatians.

Starring in the attack operation witnessed by this author was a dog named Casper, a friendly animal except when lawbreakers are around. The prized "baby" of Steinberg, he is one of the smartest furred cops on call anywhere in the world. The other three dogs of this division of the Freeport police, like Casper, all males, are named Frack, Mike and Gunner. The canines have all been repeatedly involved in real missions on occasions when the lawless meant business until one or another of the dogs caught up with them.*

The dogs at the time of this writing were all relatively young,

* All four are still on duty with the Freeport police at the time this book goes to press in 1967.

their ages ranging from twenty months to two years. Each has his own patrolman master, or handler, as in most other K-9 divisions of police throughout the world. During this refresher activity Frack and Mike, respectively the dogs of McGoldrick and Nicolino, were watching the proceedings, held on leash by McGoldrick. Gunner was on patrol in the town with his handler, Patrolman Bryan Whitty, and could not attend.

A policeman who takes on the role of assailant in this type of training is usually humorously referred to by his colleagues as the "fall guy." The fact that a policeman is involved—even one they know well—will not deter these special dogs from unswervingly obeying the orders of their handlers.

In this practice the fall guy is protected by a heavy quilted sleeve extending from the shoulder to beyond his fingertips. The dogs are trained to make for the protected arm. In some operations the dog's human quarry is protected by a heavily quilted suit covering him from neck to ankles, but such a garb was not used in this particular training session.

"It's really no great sweat, this training, it's something of a game and the dog's actually enjoy it," Steinberg said, permitting me to pat Casper's superb head. "Oh, he won't bite—he'll only attack if he's ordered to. Of course, I would not advise any hood, however tough, to get involved in such a ruckus as you have just seen, especially at night. As far as I am concerned Casper did very well. You see, to keep an unleashed dog under control in this type of 'attack agitation' is ticklish. They are excited but seem to know what their duty is. It is difficult for the dog to realize that he must not budge—whether leashed or unleashed—until the attack command is given, regardless of how threatening or how close the enemy may be."

Nicolino, grinning, walked up, removing the quilted shield from his arm.

"That Casper has some hold, but he sure breaks well, Gary," he said. "He's a real champ."

Turning to me, he added: "It looks dangerous, but as you can see, I have not been hurt at all. You have to be a little careful sometimes about your fingertips. The dogs, however, are trained so that they almost invariably make for an arm between wrist and elbow when threatened with a revolver in this fashion. I knew that Casper would obey every order. We are really the best of friends, though Mike over there is naturally my favorite."

Steinberg, a burly, handsome man in his early thirties with a fine head of dark hair, chief dog handler on the force, commented:

"From the very beginning we train our dogs against any gun-shyness. This is practically standard in all K-9 training, either in police or army, in this country or abroad. Our four dogs by now know very well what they must do with any enemy with a weapon—club, knife, revolver, rifle, you name it. Even wounded, they will fight to the death unless they receive an order to stop—to break.

"The revolver was loaded with blanks but even if it had been real ammunition Casper would have gone boring in."

Casper probably would only have inflicted superficial injury even if a real enemy had been involved, not shielded by the quilted sleeve. The dogs are trained to get a firm hold on an arm or, if necessary, lower leg or foot, and to maintain it without crushing bones or inflicting serious wounds.

The main driving force behind the K-9 organization in Freeport is a chunky, gray-haired man with keen blue eyes and an affable, casual manner. He is Chief Edward Dixon, top man in the Freeport police. Although unable to attend the refresher exercises due to the press of other duties, he provided me with varied and interesting information in a talk in his office.

"The prime function of such dogs is to track, find and corner a suspect," he said. "Once a real suspect has been found, the dog will circle him menacingly or crouch snarling in front of the man until his handler or another policeman takes over. Full-fledged attack is usually a last resort—to be executed on order. The menace of the circling dog in full view is usually quite enough. As long as the fugitive stands quietly, preferably with hands raised above the head, the dog will not touch him. Only an order will make him charge.

"Of course, a lot depends on the particular situation—they never are quite identical. If a really desperate fight is on and the policeman or policemen with the dog are under attack or felled the dog will go all out, determined to cripple the enemy. Fortunately, this does not occur often. As psychological threats— and this is one of the most important aspects of K-9 operations —our four dogs can be relied upon. They can look very, very mean, when it is necessary.

"All four are true veterans of the force with an impressive number of arrests to their credit, duly recorded," the chief added. "Every day, one or more of them is on patrol with his handler, mostly at night. We have station-wagon radio patrol cars with a special area in the back for the dogs. In spite of their daily official stints it is important to keep them sharp, especially during periods when they are not subject to real crime-hunting tests. These weekly rehearsals are necessary. The handlers also learn something each time."

Dixon is a veteran of the Freeport force, having risen to the top job after years of competent service. Although the whole police dog enterprise is relatively new to him, he is enthusiastic about it and has a keen knowledge of the problems involved. With the solid support of his 60-odd men and officers and the backing of the city government and the Freeport citizenry, this K-9 division has become a model of its kind.

While admitting that it is only a modest venture compared to those in Baltimore, Maryland, other parts of this country and abroad, Dixon and his men are justifiably proud of their furred cops. Since the dogs were enrolled in 1962, the crime graph in

Freeport has dropped steadily. The word has gone out among the lawless that the town of Freeport is an unhealthy place, especially for burglars, muggers and rapists, notably so during the hours of darkness.

On one point, Chief Dixon is very emphatic—a very important one in view of the increasing use of dogs in police work throughout the world.

"There are many poorly informed people who think that K-9 dogs of the police are naturally vicious dogs, rather carelessly acquired, and trained to be killers, a threat to all. This is utter nonsense. The dogs are carefully chosen, their pedigrees studied. Usually they are purchased from reputable kennels. Sometimes such dogs are presented to the police by private owners. All are submitted to rigorous tests before they are accepted. A dog that has a record of viciousness or shows undue savagery in early training is simply out. Each dog is assigned a special patrolman as handler, a man who loves dogs and has the required knowledge and patience. We had a fifth dog in the beginning who was a case in point. He tended to bite, heedless of orders. We could not use him. The suitable dog must basically like humans and readily become drill-perfect."

The dog training area is a large field, surrounded by a high wire mesh and steel post fence. Speckled with trees, it is located about one mile from police headquarters, in a residential area on the outskirts of the town, which has a population of about 50,000. It is still officially referred to as the Village of Freeport and these words are on the red triangular shoulder insignia of the police. It is a sprawling town rising on flat land with wide, open streets and avenues and relatively low buildings, containing various attractive residential areas bordering tree-lined thoroughfares.

There is one main gate in the field's fence which remains locked when it is not in use and is also kept closed when training is under way.

Every Tuesday afternoon, unless extremely bad weather conditions prevail, two or three of the dogs are transported by police car to the field from their kennels at headquarters. The dog area behind the front seat of such cars is enclosed in steel mesh with a rubberized flat platform. The grill is four-sided, to prevent the dogs from disturbing the driver or anyone else sitting in front. Only the driver or the handler with him possesses keys to open the back area and let the animals out.

Once on the field they are released and permitted a few minutes of play. On my visit the day was clear and cold, and they scurried around joyously, most of their attention devoted to horseplay with their handlers. Toward the stranger in their midst they were aloof but by no means inimical, occasionally brushing against my trouser legs or glancing at me speculatively. Playtime soon ended and training work began smoothly in the wake of some brisk commands from the handlers—an impressive demonstration of how these dogs have learned their manifold tasks.

After Casper had carried out his attack mission, Frack and Mike were put to the same test. Steinberg now acted as the fall guy, since one of these dogs will never attack its own handler, even in rehearsals. Then the trio showed their ability to circle a man and keep him in place—nail him—without actually attacking him, subject to all kinds of orders, such as "Sit," "Stop," "Down," "Heel," combined with hand signals.

Inevitably there were some slightly faulty performances, but the mistakes were minor. At some moments the expressions on the dogs' faces were eloquent, especially in sidewise glances at their handlers which seemed to say "Hey, boss, what do I do next?" The slightest verbal reprimand for disobedience caused an animal to grovel in shame in the grass. Invariably it would be given another try and be rewarded with the words "Good dog" which restored it to a happy state.

The dogs tackled in turn the various obstacles in the center of the field. These consist of ladders resting against fairly high platforms, sloping platforms of thin logs looking like roofs, various jumping hurdles, a long sewer pipe and a hoop. On command, Frack, Mike and Casper climbed up and down various ladders—a very difficult task for them. They then dashed up platforms and slithered down them, executed magnificent jumps across the hurdles, and crawled through sewer pipes. Inflammable substance on the hoop was ignited and each in turn leaped through it without hesitation. Such dogs must be ready to enter areas which are on fire if it is necessary.

In actuality a fugitive may seek to escape from the police by scaling a wall or fence too high for a dog to cross by itself. To cope with such a contingency, an effective team technique has been evolved. The handler bends over near the wall—which in practice is vertical—providing a kind of stepping-stone for the animal. The dog leaps on the man's back, secures new leverage in practically uninterrupted motion, and soars over a wall or alights on a roof. Obstacles of 12 feet and even higher can be overcome by one of the dogs in this manner.

In the tracking tests which followed, the remarkable noses of the animals almost immediately picked up the trail of a "fugitive" (in this case McGoldrick) who had hidden himself in bushes at one end of the field while the dogs were negotiating various obstacles. He was nailed in two minutes flat.

Another very important phase of training is teaching the animals to search for objects which might provide helpful clues to the police. A pocketbook was dropped in the grass behind a tree by one of the trainers in a deliberately furtive stroll across the field. None of the dogs was aware of this maneuver. Steinberg led Casper to the spot where the trainer had started and said, "Find." With uncanny rapidity the dog picked up the scent and headed straight for the spot where the pocketbook lay.

He returned with it in his mouth and dropped it at Steinberg's feet. A ball was dropped in another area in somewhat the same manner, and Mike promptly found it.

"Although they can really do amazing things, dogs have their limitations in this matter, which mainly depends on picking up a scent," Steinberg said. "Very many factors are involved—weather, the time that has elapsed since a person was in an area, how many persons have stamped about in the spot. If some monkey takes off in a car or on a motorcycle or bicycle, you cannot expect a dog to follow it. Perhaps he can indicate the spot where the machine left, but that is about it. There was a burglary here recently, and Gunner was put on the job somewhat belatedly. Apparently no one but the burglar had been around, but Gunner picked up a scent all right. He was off like a flash straining at the leash, Whitty panting behind him. He got his man but his handler was not very happy. It was a collie. But for the leash and Whitty's strong arm it would have probably terminated in a dog row. These Alsatians are generally polite toward each other—their own breed—but not too friendly toward other types of dogs, especially the larger ones. We try to knock this out of their heads, but it is rather difficult. Well, maybe it is natural in view of their training and the fact that Alsatians are natural-born scrappers."

On one occasion, during night hours, Freeport patrolmen stopped and questioned two suspects in a burglary that had occurred shortly before. The police were fairly certain they were guilty; they had previous records. The men insisted they were innocent. K-9 was alerted and in a few minutes Frack and his handler were at the scene of the robbery—a store.

Frack promptly picked up a scent. About midway between the store and the point where the men were being questioned the dog swerved aside from the street and scanned a vacant lot littered with various types of rubbish.

In less than a minute he pulled a revolver out from under a

pile of cans and garbage with his teeth. The two suspects could not long deny that it belonged to one of them. The fact that the dog also followed the trail from the store to the point where the two stood was further proof for the police that they were guilty. They were arrested, confessed, and eventually served time for their felony. One more arrest citation for the dogs in police headquarters' records.

The ability of dogs to pick up a scent and follow it—notably bloodhounds—has been pondered, written about and discussed for centuries. Many aspects of this are still a mystery to experts. Effective action where a dog arrives on the scene early, knows the scent of a person or animal, or has sniffed a piece of apparel worn by a man, woman or child, are fairly understandable in view of acute olfactory organs and natural hunting instincts. This is particularly so when the dog has to operate in terrain where there are not too many human or animal scents and the animal is tracking while a scent is relatively fresh. But this situation is rather the exception than the rule, especially in police work with canines. Frequently a dog has to pick up a scent from among a vast number of others, confronted with an acute problem of selection, the scent old, terrain and weather unfavorable. Time and again the animals have picked up the right trail, even when their foreknowledge of the particular scent sought is practically nil. This ability, especially among trained trackers, still stumps the experts and is much harder to comprehend. Following a trail through busy city streets does not baffle all canine trackers. The extraordinary exploits of Italy's world-famous Dox, a champion of champions, are worth noting in this regard. The giant Alsatian—whose career is discussed later in this book —did on many occasions, according to all evidence, pursue elusive scents through some of the busiest streets of Rome.

Having satisfactorily completed their various refresher tests, Frack, Mike and Casper were permitted to romp again on the field for a few minutes and then were ordered back into their car cages. This they did obediently, all of them a trifle fatigued by their arduous workouts.

"They did well today, they are full of beans in this coldish weather," Steinberg commented before the ride back to headquarters in one of the two special dog patrol cars. "You know, they're like us. They have their good days and their bad ones. In addition, each dog has its own particular talents; one is better in this, another in that. Full obedience to commands, or at least proof of a sincere desire to obey, is a must, however, for all of them."

Questioned on the effect of unfavorable weather conditions on these regular refresher exercises, Steinberg pointed to a large building just beyond the training field.

"If, for example, a blizzard hits, we can either change the date or use that armory you see over there. As far as snow is concerned, these babies eat it up—literally. Barring impossible conditions, we just go to the field as usual. If snow is around in playtime periods we pelt them with snowballs or have them chase after them—great fun for all of us. They do quite well with a trail in snow too.

"There is one exercise we did not do today which should be mentioned. Cars are repeatedly involved in all kinds of cases, generally stolen ones. They can nail these too. They know what occupants might do, what exits are available. If we have a suspect in a car, after it has been stopped we post a dog on guard. We leave one door open usually if a limousine is involved. The dog is outside this open door looking inside steadily. Should a suspect try to start the motor or make any other suspicious move, the dog will growl menacingly. If anyone in the car gets out, the dog or dogs are after him like a flash.

"In one case, a suspect tried to escape while patrolmen were some distance away and were not looking at the car. Mike was on guard. The man, seated in the back, made a sudden move for the door farthest from the dog outside. Mike was on the alert. When the man disregarded his menacing growl, Mike just sailed in and glared and howled in the man's face. An angry Alsatian's open mouth and eyes close to your face—not very nice, rough. When the police came up the man was unhurt but had had it."

No untoward incident occurred on the way back to the police station. On arrival, the dogs were taken out on leash and lead back to their kennels.

The building housing police headquarters and also mayoral offices is a rather large, red brick structure alongside a small park. This is home for the dogs, although from time to time a handler will take his animal to his own home for a brief change of residence.

At headquarters each dog has its own individual and roomy kennel. Each kennel is enclosed by a steel wire grill about 8 feet high. These are about 9 by 14 feet, giving each dog an area to move around in when not in the kennel. Each enclosure carries a wooden nameplate with the name of the dog printed in large letters on it. The wooden kennel house is provided with a thermostatic device which ensures a suitable flow of heat inside the kennel should the weather become suddenly cold in spring or autumn. If severe winter weather prevails all four are shifted to wooden stall-like kennels in a room nearby in the headquarters' basement.

The kennels and their enclosures face on a small courtyard with one gate, which usually is locked. In the middle of the courtyard—looking oddly out of place—is an old-fashioned enamel bathtub. Here the dogs are given a thorough scrubbing with soap and water at regular times by their handlers. In the basement area is a special room containing various types of K-9 equipment. This includes collars, leashes, medicines, and bags containing varied dog victuals which complement their daily ration of raw meat. All sleep very comfortably on cedarwood shavings which, it has been found, repel fleas and other insects. Frack, Mike, Gunner and Casper receive regular checkups by a local veterinarian and are never sent out on regular rounds if ailing in any way.

The four handlers are policemen like any others on the 60-man force but their assignment with the dogs is a full-time one. Each man and dog form a team and they operate as such in a rotating system of patrols. The men receive some extra pay for their special job but also volunteer for a considerable amount of off-duty work involving the animals, such as weekly refresher exercises, grooming the animals, ensuring sufficient off-duty exercise and the like.

On our tour of police headquarters, Chief Dixon went into a small room and pointed to an assortment of sport equipment, all brand-new, stashed in corner. It consisted of two football helmets, a basketball, two tennis rackets, and some other objects.

"Offhand, I would say about two hundred dollars' worth," the chief commented. "Stolen stuff, all of it, but going back to the store very soon, thanks to Mike.

"A young punk broke into a local sports store a few nights ago and took off with this stuff in a bag. One of my men on late night duty spotted him but just a few seconds too late. This punk could run real fast and our man knew he could not catch up with him. But he was able almost immediately to get in touch with a patrol car containing Mike and his handler.

"Mike was put on the trail and the thief didn't stand a chance after that—even if he had been an Olympic champion runner. The burglar tried to climb over a fairly high fence but Mike got one of the guy's feet in his teeth and held on. When Nicolino and the other policeman came up the fugitive was standing very still against the wall with Mike watching him. Mike drew some blood that time but it was nothing serious. The boy's in jail now and I am sure does not want to get in a hassle with police dogs again."

The dogs work in regular shifts with their handlers, giving Freeport 24-hour coverage, with one or more animals on patrol either in radio cars or afoot. The emphasis is, logically, on night duty when law infractions occur most frequently. Also dogs are particularly useful "eyes" for policemen at night, particularly in ill-lit or dark areas which need scanning.

"Our shifts in K-9 are scheduled so that two handlers and two dogs are on duty from six P.M. to two A.M. Each stint is for eight hours. The first night duty tour is from four P.M. to midnight. Another team is on tour from six P.M. to two A.M. When the pair that started at four P.M. leave at midnight another team takes its place from midnight to eight A.M. During the daytime hours, when trouble is less likely, a team is on duty from eight A.M. to four P.M. In rotation each team gets its share of the more pleasant eight A.M. to four P.M. stint—at least more pleasant for the man involved.

"Naturally, this schedule is not absolutely fixed and can be changed if circumstances demand it. Even during daytime, when only one dog and handler are on duty, the whole division can be put into action in short order."

Dixon pointed out that patrolmen other than the handlers can use the dogs if necessary, since the dogs respect the uniform and know that they are friends. However, it is always best to have a specific handler in action. The animals will obey the other men but not as faultlessly as their own masters.

"The dogs are always worked on leashes and only released when it is necessary to catch a lawbreaker," Dixon pointed out. "We are strict about this but, naturally, it is up to the handler to decide in an emergency. In a general sense something criminal and dangerous to the policeman or the residents must be afoot before any dog is ordered into attack pattern, either on leash or free. For example, it would be just out of order to use a dog to intimidate some harmless drunk staggering about either in day-time or at night, unless he should suddenly prove to be a real menace, weapon in hand."

Almost invariably the K-9 teams are assigned to sections of the township where crime is most prevalent. In Freeport, as in many other American communities, these are the areas where Negroes live. Here law infractions tend to be more frequent than elsewhere due to economic and other factors which are profoundly troubling the entire nation.

Neither the Freeport dogs nor police dogs elsewhere are trained to dislike Negroes or persons of any particular color. In fact, scientific research has proven with little doubt that dogs see a black, gray and white world, devoid of the color distinctions provided by the human eye.

Police dogs are extremely effective in riot control in some instances. The mere presence of a K-9 dog has a powerful psychological effect on a crowd which the police want to control. The problem of using dogs in this capacity is a very touchy one. In recent years there has been considerable angry public reaction to riot or crowd control abetted by dogs. One of the most glaring incidents occurred in Birmingham, Alabama, when civil rights demonstrators, most of them Negroes, were harried by police dogs. Many demonstrators were bitten, some of them seriously. As a result, Negro leaders and many white persons oppose the organization of any type of K-9 unit in any community.

The Chicago, Illinois, police, which operate an important K-9 unit, officially announced that dogs no longer would be used in riot control following disorders in a Puerto Rican neighborhood. These riots came after a patrolman had shot a Puerto Rican in the leg during the summer of 1966. Dogs were subsequently used in attempts to quell rioting. One Puerto Rican was bitten and the anger among the Puerto Ricans prompted the police decision to avoid the use of dogs in the future. Scot-

land Yard of London, which has the largest K-9 contingent in
the world, flatly opposes riot or crowd control with canine aid.
The best-trained dog, British officials hold, tends to become
overexcited and confused when tackling a crowd, prone to bite
suddenly and heedless of command.

Some police officials are of the opinion that dogs can prove
extremely helpful in handling disorderly crowds or potentially
dangerous groups, providing they are small. But the animals
should always be under full control—psychological deterrents,
not attack tools designed to draw blood. In any case, most experts agree, a dog's skills are better used in other domains of law
enforcement.

While not commenting in any way on this issue, Chief Dixon
pointed out that his department's dogs had proved very useful
in coping with threatening crowds of disorderly youngsters in
Freeport. Such incidents did not involve anything like a Negro
march or demonstration, merely rough elements bent on trouble. In one case a minor riot was impending when the dogs,
firmly held on leash, came on the scene. Kept at a safe distance
by their handlers, their presence was quite enough. The crowd
dispersed promptly without a single person having been injured.

The Freeport police chief shares the belief of virtually all K-9
experts that the German shepherd dog is the stellar breed for
police work. The name Alsatian is something of a misnomer for
this dog. It was coined during World War I by Allied troops,
who were using many German shepherds in battle zones, to
dispel any idea that they were German animals. A very slim link
with a type of dog found in Alsace was used as a justification for
the appellation. The name has stuck, however, and is accepted
as correct by dog breeders.

The Alsatians have a high degree of intelligence and their
senses of smell and hearing are excellent. They are a relatively
new breed—distinctly a German evolution. A pure breed of this

type of dog did not exist prior to the late 1800's. It was at this time that German breeders began to mingle various strains of wolflike shepherd dogs to create the handsome and alert dog which is familiar to all dog lovers, especially in Europe. All Alsatians in K-9 units have German names in their pedigrees, their ancestry generally making them true aristocrats of their kind.

Alsatians function well in almost any climate, except possibly extremely hot areas. The dog has a double coat to protect it in all kinds of weather: a harsh, straight outer coat of medium length and a dense, woolly undercoat. Color may range from black to white. The most characteristic colors are wolf-gray or beige and black.

Of course other types of dogs have been and are being used in police work, such as Labrador retrievers, Doberman pinschers and even Airedales, but they have never quite matched the Alsatian for police operations and for special guard duty.

The sleek, fast Doberman has all the keen faculties necessary for police operations but it is somewhat unpredictable, slow to mature, frequently having a vicious streak. It is prone to go in for the kill with a slash at the throat and is not as impeccably obedient as the German shepherd. However, Dobermans are being used effectively to guard big department stores, such as Macy's in New York City, the biggest department store in the world. This is simple night guard duty to foil after-hours pilferers and does not have all the complex angles of police work.

There are many Dobermans among the dogs enrolled by the American armed forces but again this work involves a training more aggressive than that of police work and designed for different conditions. In World War II, notably in the Pacific, the scouting activities of these dogs operating with attacking American troops in jungle fighting time and again meant finis for Japanese infantrymen.

The Labradors, among the larger canines, have given splendid service, principally in England. The most famous of these was London's Ben, dog idol of all Britishers. Ben evolved his own unique "attack pattern." He would charge up to a malefactor, shove his massive head and shoulders between the man's legs, and with violent twists cause the man to fall. Then he would solemnly keep his victim under surveillance until his handler came up. These Labradors, however, have a little too much friendliness in their makeup and are not as speedy as the trimmer Alsatian.

Not all outstanding dogs in special operations are necessarily purebred. Chips, the most famous American war dog of World War II, certainly was not a "blueblood." His father was a husky and his mother a mixture of collie and German shepherd. Single-handedly Chips routed an Italian machine-gun unit in Sicilian fighting, was recommended for the Distinguished Service Cross, won the Silver Star, met President Franklin D. Roosevelt and Prime Minister Winston Churchill and bit the finger of a future American President, then his supreme military commander, General Dwight D. Eisenhower. The bite was not serious.

In acquiring dogs, police do not purchase puppies because in this stage the basic characteristics or aptitudes of the dog cannot be foreseen. The preferred bracket for acceptance is from six to fourteen months. The basic training period lasts usually fourteen weeks. Kindness and patience on the part of the handlers are the keynote of such training. Some sternness is required at times but never is severe punishment involved. This would be quite senseless. Such action tends to snuff out a dog's spirit, engendering fear and timidity. If a dog cannot meet requirements during training it is marked off as a loss through no fault of its own and is returned to civilian life. Usually it is returned to its original owner or a new, suitable owner is found for the animal.

During the training, dogs are taught not to accept food from strangers in any form. This lessens the risk of their being poisoned by ill-intentioned persons. The same applies to food which may be found in streets, houses or fields, and water and any other liquids which are not on their regular menu. This requires considerable patience on the part of trainers. The dogs are confronted with food or liquid they are not supposed to touch. A sharp "No!" repeated again and again, sometimes complemented by a mild cuff, is usually effective eventually. Frequent stroking or petting by strangers, young or adult, is discouraged by the police. A certain distrust toward strangers is desirable in such animals, much more so than in the case of civilian pets. However, the well-trained dog does not automatically snap at a hand extended in a friendly gesture by someone he does not know.

Generally, the police prefer a grouping of male dogs. It has been found by some police that the presence of a female dog may cause trouble, provoking jealousies and fights among the males.

Handlers assigned to police dogs are always volunteers. They are not ordered to do this highly specialized work. Men between the ages of thirty and forty are preferred. They must have a proven liking for dogs and have acquired a sound knowledge of such animals and their characteristics before they are assigned. There are exceptions of course, like that of Giovanni Maimone, master of Dox. A policeman in Turin, Italy, Maimone, who knew dogs well and loved them, acquired Dox as a puppy without a "by our leave" from his superiors. The whole procedure was very irregular but the results in this case were spectacular.

Usually a dog's span of useful service in police or army work is 10 to 11 years. They are considered too old for such arduous duty after their eleventh birthday. An eleven-year-old canine, according to the 7 to 1 ratio in comparing their age to that of human beings, is about seventy-seven years old. There are exceptions, however. Dox was ninety-eight human years old when he was retired, still functioning efficiently. In very many cases handlers become so attached to their animals that they elect to care for them in the dog's declining years following retirement. A shining example of this was Maimone's devotion to Dox until the time when "Il Gigante" (The Giant) went on his last journey.

Many a handler has his own private pet dog at home, not subjected to any special training. Patrolman Steinberg of Freeport has an Alsatian pet dog in his home named Flash. Flash and Casper are the best of friends whenever they meet. McGoldrick goes a step further—his hobby is breeding dogs.

The designation "K-9" is logical in view of the pronunciation of the word defining dogs—canines—in the English language. It is official in this country both for army and police dog units. In England, France, Germany, Italy, and elsewhere different designations such as dog division or department are applied. The letter and numeral "K-9," however, are thoroughly familiar to all persons engaged in this type of work.

Employment of trained dogs by the police and armed forces has expanded markedly throughout the world since the turn of the century, largely owing to two world wars and increasingly serious crime problems.* At present many cities in the United States have K-9 divisions on duty, including Baltimore, Washington, D.C., Chicago and St. Louis, Missouri. Unfortunately, there is no national or international body dedicated to collating statistics and general information on K-9 operations. This makes it difficult to provide the reader with overall information. The United States armed forces have a large number of trained dogs of different breeds on duty giving valuable service as guards at depots and missile sites and as scouts, messengers and aides to medical corpsmen seeking wounded or injured per-

---

* The remarkable achievements of Seeing Eye dogs, involving specialized training, will not be covered in this book.

sons. Exact information could not be obtained on this matter by the author.

Many police departments formed K-9 units and eventually disbanded them even though the dogs had done good work. Increased mechanized mobility and improved telegraphic, radio and telephone communication in police operations has been partly responsible for cessation of K-9 work. The city of Ghent, Belgium, which was a pioneer in the use of police dogs at the turn of the century, stopped this operation completely in 1938, according to a letter received from the police department of that city. It has not reinstituted such a department. Norwegian police have 80 trained dogs enrolled at this writing. Most of them are Alsatians, the others Dobermans and Rottweilers.

"In Norway the police has been using dogs since 1920," the Oslo police stated in a letter. "Both dogs and men, working as teams, have carried out many successful missions together. In Oslo we have now regular dog patrols night and day, with special cars available for swift transportation.

"From our experience it does sometimes seem as if a dog thinks just like a human being," the Oslo letter commented. "However, the dog must be trained to do certain things if an operation is to be successful. It often happens that a dog gets confused when he is confronted with a task which is totally novel to him.

"One of our most remarkable canines was named 'Jarl.' He died in 1945, thirteen years old. During his final year of duty he tracked down his last murderer. This man killed two persons, set fire to their house and then fled to wild mountain terrain. Jarl and his handler joined police seeking him and he was cornered, largely through the tracking skill of this exceptional dog. Jarl came upon him as he was crouching in the forest, armed with a loaded rifle. Jarl tackled him so swiftly and skillfully that he did not have the chance to fire a shot."

As in all affairs involving humans and dogs, there have been numerous diverting incidents, especially in cases where "missing" children are really not lost at all. Calls for help in this type of incident are frequent all over the world and police dogs prove very helpful.

"We've had a couple of these in Freeport," Patrolman Steinberg said. "Casper and I handled one. A very nervous woman asking us to come over quick and find her four-year-old girl. She said she had been looking all through the house but no results. So we went over and Casper roamed around sniffing a bit outside after having smelled a piece of the child's clothing. Just how he reached a conclusion I don't know, but he just went and sat down in front of the main door and looked at the house. Casper is no fool and I asked the woman to take another look-see. The dog was right. The kid was in the house, quite okay, hiding in a closet. Casper and the kid closed the incident with a friendly handshake. The kid also got a big, friendly lick on the face, because Casper likes children."

Plainclothes men sometimes pose a problem for police dogs, in view of their special respect for a police uniform. In one incident in one of our cities everything turned out fine in a case involving a detective—that is, fine for everybody but the police.

During a night patrol an unleashed police dog cornered a burglar in a deserted area and began circling him menacingly, waiting for his handler to come upon the scene.

The handler was some distance away but a detective in civilian attire was nearby in a car and was within eyeshot of the dog and the thief. He promptly got out of the car drawing his revolver. He knew the dog and somewhat carelessly believed that it would not be disturbed by his presence since it had the fugitive under control. When he drew near, revolver in hand, the dog immediately widened its sphere of action to include the detective. The dog had him disarmed and flattened against a wall when the handler ran up. The burglar, however, had vanished and was not recaptured.

The use of "remote control" dogs—particularly in rugged, country terrain—has been successfully tried in England, Australia and various countries other than the United States. A small, specially built radio receiving set is attached to a dog's collar. The handler, equipped with a portable transmitting set, can control the dog with commands over distances where hand signals and shouted orders would be quite useless. In less complex operations handlers have followed a trail with their dog on leash using a walkie-talkie to inform police not on the scene of various developments in the hunt.

In the Swiss Alps helicopters have been used to transport rescue dogs in a hurry to areas where a disaster has occurred. These animals, known as the "avalanche dogs," have been trained as rescue units by the Swiss Army. Some of the dogs, equipped with their own parachutes, have been landed in very inaccessible spots along with parachuted handlers to undertake rescue work. In all cases of avalanches involving humans or livestock, the dogs have proven of immense value in locating points where the living or the dead have been engulfed.

A detailed picture of the police problems in which K-9 dogs proved valuable is contained in statements published by the Kansas City, Missouri, police department, which has an important K-9 corps. One of these statements, applicable to other K-9 operations, says:

The adoption of trained dogs for police work does not depend upon the size of the department but upon prevailing police problems. The following types of crime have dropped as much as 50% in areas where dogs have been assigned:

Peeping Toms. Homosexual offenses. Crowd disturbances. Juvenile problems. Disorderly persons. Car strips. Muggings. Family fights. Assault and burglaries. Prowlers. Child molesters. . . . Vandalism. Dogs also have proven useful in handling pedestrian traffic at major fires and controlling crowds at disaster scenes, handling parade crowds, helping the police in vice raids, patrolling parks and locating lost children and senile persons or state hospital patients.

𒀀𒅗𒇷𒂊𒈾𒊏𒋫

*Assyrian inscription about
dogs in cuneiform meaning
"captures enemies"*

> *If you pick up a starving dog and make him pros-
> perous, he will not bite you. That is the principal
> difference between a dog and a man.*
>
> —MARK TWAIN

2

Dog of Epirus

A DOG, a king and two murderers were
the main actors in a drama of long ago which has given us the
first recorded account of canine criminal detection work. It was
reported in some detail by an unknown Greek historian and
occurred some 2,300 years ago during the reign of King Pyrrhus
of Epirus (300 to 272 B.C.), ruler over territory that today lies
partly in northwestern Greece and partly in southern Yugo-
slavia. The story is as follows:

. . . A certain slave for some unknown reason had been done to
death by two men, when they met him on a lonely road. His dog,
who was with him and the sole witness, remained by the body. The
king [Pyrrhus] passed that way on a royal progress, and, observing

the animal by the side of the corpse, bade his charioteers halt. "Bury the body," he commanded, "and bring the dog to me."

Some time elapsed: the dog remained with his new master, and accompanied him when he went to a review of his troops. As two of the soldiers marched smartly past, the animal flew at them with such fury that he all but tore them to pieces. No further evidence was needed, for, in order to escape from the dog, the criminals confessed their guilt.

The historian's account ends here. Presumably the criminals were executed then and there. What kind of dog was involved is not recorded. Probably it was a smaller type of animal and tried to defend its master when he was attacked but was beaten off with clubs or other weapons.

This king has a special niche in history. To this day the words "Pyrrhic victory" are used to describe a battle gained at too great a cost of life, such as that won by Pyrrhus over the Romans at Asculum in 279 B.C. It is said that when the monarch died and was being cremated one of his many dogs jumped into the flames to join its master in death.

"That's where the money is" was the classic reply given by one of the most famous robbers of modern times, "Willy" Sutton, when he was asked why he specialized in the robbing of banks. In ancient times this statement could very well have applied to pagan temples and Christian monasteries and churches. Storehouses for valuables of many types, including gold and silver artifacts, many of them studded with priceless gems, they were a constant lure to thieves. Dogs proved to be invaluable guardians of such edifices.

One temple dog which gained fame in ancient Athens was named Cupparas. An outstanding achievement of this dog has been cited by the noted French essayist and philosopher Michel de Montaigne. It apparently occurred in the first century of the Christian era.

On guard during the night, Cupparas spotted a thief carrying away some loot and began to bark at him as he ran from the temple.

Seeing he could not awaken the Sextons, or Temple-keepers, the dog followed the man whither so-ever he went [Montaigne recounted]. When daylight came, he kept himself aloof, but never lost sight of him; if he offered him (the dog) meat, he utterly refused it: but if any person chanced to come by, on them he fawned with wagging of his tail and took whatever they offered him; if the thief stayed to rest himself, he also stayed in the same place: the news of this dog being come to the Temple-keepers, they as they went along, enquiring of the dog's hair and color, pursued the track so long, that at last they found both the dog and the thief in the City of Cromyon, whom they brought back to Athens. And the judges in acknowledgment of the dog's good office, at the City's charge appointed him for his sustenance a certain daily measure of corn and enjoined the priests of the Temple carefully to look unto him. Plutarch affirms this story to be most true and to have happened in his time.

Archaeological findings show with certainty that the dog was a companion of man tens of thousands of years before the dawn of history. A drawing of hunting dogs, discovered on the wall of a cave of the Paleolithic era, has been estimated to be 50,000 years old. In another discovery, scientists found the skeleton of a young girl surrounded by the bones of four dogs, the remains believed to be from the Cro-Magnon era, some 25,000 years old. The dog is mentioned or portrayed in carvings or paintings since the earliest centuries of recorded history, which goes back some 6,000 years.

Mystery still surrounds the evolution of the dog, just what were its forebears and how the animal developed. It is considered by many historians to be the oldest domesticated animal, the first to become a friend of mankind.

"From a zoological point of view the dog (Canis) is not ancient for, although a doglike form existed some 20,000,000 years ago, it is doubtful whether a partially domesticated dog existed earlier than the late Pleistocene Age," Clifford L. B. Hubbard, an English authority on dog lore, asserts. "This would make it not more than about a million years old; a million years is not a very great deal of time in the history of the animal kingdom. So it is important from the very outset that we recognize the true dog as a relatively recent creature."

It is generally believed that a small creature much like the civet cat known as Tomarctos is the common ancestor of all dogs. This animal, which lived some 15,000,000 years ago, evolved from earlier animals such as the Miacis, Cynodictis and Cynodesmus, the latter a creature of the early Miocene period. Tomarctos was the ancestor of the wolf. The dog we know today, it is believed, has the wolf or the jackal in its genealogy. Of all the animals existing today the wolf is undoubtedly that most similar to the dog.

A perceptive statement regarding the dog's value as a loyal companion was attributed to the Persian god of very ancient times, Ahura Mazda: "Self-clothed, watchful, wakeful and sharp-toothed, born to watch men's goods."

According to a legend stemming from early Christian times, it was a dog that may have saved all other animals from drowning and as a result its nose has been cold ever since. The legend says that a dog sealed a leak in Noah's Ark by putting its snout into it and keeping it there for many days, its nostrils chilled by the torrential rains of the Biblical deluge. Dogs as such come in for little commendation, however, in the Bible. Of the 40 to 50 references to dogs in the Bible the great majority are derogatory.

Perhaps it is a merciful thing that the dog's span of life on this earth is a short one. Man's cruelty toward this useful and incredibly loyal animal is a dark record.

Untold thousands were used as sacrifices to pagan gods, the

methods of execution cruel. Primitive tribes still sacrifice them today. Dogs of all types were pitted against other animals and armed men in bloody "entertainments" in the Colosseum and other ancient Roman arenas. The Irish wolfhound, the world's tallest dog, imported to the Imperial City from the north, was a famous competitor in these arenas. They were the only dogs with recorded victories over the lion and the elephant. The Romans said that three of them were a match for a bear and four for a lion. Many perished in the combats with animals and also with armed gladiators. At various times in history dogs, on some occasions protected by special chain mail or steel plate armor and equipped with spiked collars, were launched against cavalry and foot in big battles. Very few survived such ordeals and those wounded were left to die on the field in agony.

Although matters have improved somewhat in modern times, the abandonment of dogs to their fate by callous owners has been and is a commonplace occurrence throughout the world. The sight of a lost dog in a city street or elsewhere is a tragic one and the fate of those canines not lucky enough to find a new, more kindly master often is heartrending. Creation of societies for the prevention of cruelty to animals has naturally greatly alleviated suffering among dogs. But such dedicated people are not operating everywhere.

A particularly vicious threat confronts virtually all dogs, even today: the activities of dog kidnappers, sinister individuals who capture any dog they can, treat it shamefully, and then sell the animal for use in medical experiments. No doubt readers can recall photographs published in recent years in this country showing dogs dead or succumbing to starvation in the filthy "kennels" operated by one of these kidnappers.

During the two world conflicts of this century dogs were used in large numbers in battle zones but not as ruthlessly as in ancient times. They were immensely valuable in carrying messages from one position to another. Or they aided medical units in finding wounded men in forest and field and in the ruins of buildings. Thousands of soldiers have owed their lives to the fact that they were located quickly by these four-footed friends. Although not used for offensive purposes, the dog casualty list was high since they frequently were fully exposed to rifle and other fire.

When the Spaniards came to the New World, they brought numerous large dogs with them as combatants and guards. These dogs, which included bloodhounds, were used to frighten hostile Indians or to attack them. Many of the Indians, as far as is known, had never before seen such animals. They apparently were as new and frightening to them as the horses of the new arrivals.

Juan Ponce de León brought with him a big bloodhound named Becerrico. This dog must have been a special terror to the Indians according to an old Spanish account about his activities.

He made wonderful havoc among these people and therefore had one share and a half of what was taken and it was allowed to him as well in gold, slaves and other things as was due to one who carried a crossbow.

The courage, reliability and loyalty of dogs are noted in a historical account of an engagement between the Athenians and the Corinthians during the Peloponnesian War (431–404 B.C.):

The Corinthians, too, used dogs for purposes of defense. The citadel of Corinth had a guard of 50 placed in boxes by the seashore. Taking advantage of a dark night, the Greeks [Athenians] with whom they were at war disembarked on the coast. The garrison were asleep after an orgy, the dogs alone kept watch, the fifty [dog] pickets fell on the enemy, like lions; all but one were casualties. Sorter, sole survivor, retiring from the conflict, fled to the town to give warning and roused the drunken soldiers, who came forth to battle. To him alone were the honors of victory, and the grateful town presented to him a collar with the inscription: "Sorter, Defender and Savior of Corinth" and erected a monument engraved with his name and those of the 49 heroes who fell.

Possibly the Indians attacked by the Spaniards of Ponce de León had never seen a dog, but he certainly was a familiar animal to Indians of this country in the past centuries. Dogs always were present in Indian encampments and villages, proving invaluable sentries who sounded the alarm when an enemy was on the prowl. They were very useful to white men in the wilderness as well.

The Indians had high respect for the courage of dogs although they generally accorded them indifferent care and frequently slaughtered them and ate them with relish. The Dakotas used to kill dogs and eat their livers raw before going on the warpath, believing that this action would endow a warrior with the courage of these animals.

One of the notable Indian legends about dogs was spun by Potawatomi storytellers. They said that a woman had been weaving a basket on the moon since time immemorial. If she ever completed the basket it would lead to total destruction of our planet. But each time the basket neared completion a dog chewed it up. This was asserted to be the cause of celestial eclipses.

Ethiopian tribesmen in Africa at one time were said to have made a dog their king. The animal—a lucky one in any dog's language—resided in his own royal hut, guarded day and night by picked warriors, slaves attending to all his wants. The dog had his own bevy of canine "concubines" and ruled in a very special manner. A wag or wags of his tail meant approval, a bark or barks meant disapproval and a growl meant intense fury.

Such a growl constituted a sentence of death for anyone haled before the "dog throne" for trial.

One of the Egyptian gods, Anubis, had the head of a dog and the body of a man. An ancient Egyptian locality was known as the City of Dogs, its Greek name Cynopolis. According to Greek mythology a fearsome dog, three-headed Cerberus, was constantly on guard at the gates of the nether regions.

The animal is the subject of some odd proverbs besides such familiar sayings as "leading a dog's life" and he "died like a dog." Some of the most unusual ones come from Wales and from Devon and Northamptonshire in England. One of them is to the effect that a dog can be helpful in curing a common cold. This RX goes:

A cure for a cough is to put the hair of a patient's head between two slices of buttered bread and give it to a dog.

Others are:

It is unlucky to meet a barking dog in the morning.

If a dog runs between a woman's legs her husband is going to beat her.

It is lucky to be eaten by dogs because you will drive a fine team in the next world.

To stop a dog howling at night turn your shoes upside down.

If the last saying is valid, it might have been wise for Romero and his Spaniards to have gone into action in stockinged feet in the historic nocturnal raid recounted in the next chapter.

*By the pricking of my thumbs something wicked
this way comes.*

—SHAKESPEARE, *Macbeth*

3

The Hunters and the Hunted

THEIR shirts white blobs in the gloom, the 600 Spanish infantrymen left their encampment near the walled city of Mons shortly before midnight and snaked in steady cadence toward the village of Hermigny where the "heretics" slumbered. It was the night of September 11, 1572.

Seasoned killers all, the warriors advanced in menacing silence, eyes alert under the curving rims of their morion helmets. The blow must fall swiftly, surprise was imperative; these were key factors in any *encamisada*. Each man had been stripped down to boots, light clothing, steel corselets and helmets to insure maximum marching facility. All were armed to the teeth, however, with sword, poniard, pistol and arquebus, the ponderous musket of those times. None were on horseback since a horse might betray them with a sudden neigh or snort or scrape of hoof on stone. In the van of the column marched Julian Romero, one of the most renowned captains in the armies of His Most Catholic Majesty King Philip II of Spain, mightiest monarch in the world.

Romero and all his men wore their shirts over their body armor so that they could distinguish each other in the nighttime, especially so in a fight. The word *encamisada* almost invariably applied to a swift, stealthy nocturnal raid with a fairly small force. *Encamisada* means roughly "in your shirt," and this method of identification was evolved and used by the Spaniards in very many attacks of this type.

The stakes were high on this fateful night in the struggle of the 1500's known as the great revolt of the Netherlands. Romero's orders were explicit: bring back Prince William of Orange, dead or alive.

Illustrious Prince William, also known to history as William the Silent, was the No. 1 foe of the Duke of Alva, then Spanish overlord in the Lowlands, which we know today as Belgium and Holland. The people of Holland revere his name as much as we cherish that of George Washington. Tyrannous Spanish action in religious and other matters had sparked the conflict, one of the most bitter and bloody in all history. No quarter was asked, none given. What arquebus ball, crossbow quarrel or cold steel did not finish, the racks and bonfires of the Spanish Inquisition did.

On this night William's tent was in the center of his encampment at the village of Hermigny. The Spanish column started secretly from the village of Florian and headed for the enemy encampment, about two miles distant. Both villages were on the outskirts of Mons, 50-odd miles southwest of Brussels, capital of today's Belgium. The bulk of William's troops, the majority German mercenaries, were at Hermigny but the encampment was a sprawling one and not all were concentrated near the prince's tent. William had brought his force to the area in a desperate plan to break the tightening Spanish siege of Protestants in Mons.

As he advanced on Hermigny, Romero had good reason for full confidence in his men. Spanish infantrymen were the best in the world at that time and every one of his troopers was a picked volunteer. The raid had been carefully planned. Except for the raiders involved, only a few officers in the Spanish besieging force knew of this particular plan. The night was moonless, the terrain generally familiar to the raiders. Everything augured well for a devastating blow, an encamisada that might end all encamisadas in this conflict.

Romero knew that the foe would have sentries on duty but that was routine and all his men were specialists in liquidating such guardians.

There was, however, one sentry in their path that they did not count upon. This sentry, a nonhuman, was very alert.

It was a dog—the favorite spaniel of Prince William.

The Spaniards fell on the sentries in their path like phantoms and cut their throats before any one of them could let out a warning yell. Then they stormed into the enemy encampment, yelling like fiends, swords thrusting and slicing, arquebuses blasting, pistols cracking, rousing most of their opponents from slumber. While the majority of his force spread chaos at several points in the enemy camp, massacring as they went, Romero heeded specific orders from Don Fredrico of Toledo, Spanish commander in the Mons area. Accompanied by some 80 men, he headed directly for the prime target—the prince's tent.

The spaniel was in the tent curled up on the bed next to his beloved master. The dog was in the light sleep of his species; the prince's slumber was deep. The first shout outside fully awakened the animal. He sensed somehow that something abnormal was under way. Wisely he did not rush out of the tent barking loudly. There was something smarter to be done.

What befell on this night is best described in the words the great American historian, John Lothrop Motley (1814–1877) in his book *The Rise of the Dutch Republic.*

The whole army [of William] was surprised and for a moment powerless, while, for two hours long, from one o'clock in the morning [of the 12th] until three, the Spaniards butchered their forces, hardly aroused from their sleep, ignorant by how small a force they had been thus suddenly surprised and unable in the confusion to distinguish between friend and foe.

The boldest, led by Julian Romero in person, made at once for the Prince's tent. His guards and he himself were in profound sleep, but a small spaniel, who always passed the night on his bed, was a more faithful sentinel.

The creature sprang forward, barking furiously at the sound of hostile footsteps, and scratching his master's face with his paws. There was but just time for the Prince to mount a horse which was ready saddled and to effect his escape through the darkness before his enemies sprang into the tent. His servants were cut down, his master of the horse, and two of his secretaries who gained their saddles a moment later, all lost their lives; and but for the little dog's watchfulness, William of Orange, upon whose shoulders the whole weight of his country's fortunes depended, would have been led within a week to an ignominious death. To his dying day the Prince ever afterwards kept a spaniel of the same race in his bed-chamber.

The Spaniards were able to withdraw in the glare of burning tents before their confused foes, far outnumbering them, realized how small the raiding force was. Six hundred of the prince's men were massacred. Only 60 Spaniards were killed. What happened to the little spaniel is not recorded. It probably was butchered. A few years later, the great patriot prince was killed by an assassin coveting Spanish promises of large cash rewards to anyone slaying the Dutch champion.

In the same century three dogs of the same breed sought to save their master but could not change the course of history. Their lord was King Henri III of France, last of the Valois. The spaniels, named Liline, Titi and Mimi, were his favorite lapdogs. One day a vengeful monk, named Jacques Clément, a member of one of the factions inimical to the king in the bitter religious quarrels of that time, succeeded in entering the monarch's chamber in the palace of Saint-Cloud under false pretenses. Although accustomed to the arrival of various personages seeking royal audience, the dogs on this occasion did not limit themselves to the customary snappish barking but attacked the monk immediately. The king stupidly called them off and asked the intruder what he desired. Those were his last words. The monk rushed forward and plunged a poniard into the king's heart, killing him instantly.

The dogs, only temporarily quieted, resumed their attack, barking wildly. Sensing that something untoward was afoot, guards then rushed into the room and killed the monk with sword thrusts.

Although these episodes involving spaniels highlight alert animal guardianship, some relentless sleuthing by a dog is involved in one of the most famous dog stories of all time. It dates back to the Middle Ages in France, the setting a somber forest, a royal palace and an arena in Paris.

The accomplishment of this dog, believed to have been named Hercules, was in the best of traditions of police dog detection work although special K-9 training for dogs was not known at that time. The dog presumably was a cross between some type of wolfhound and a mastiff. He is the hero of a legendary account which many historians believe stemmed from an actual occurrence that took place in Paris, France, or its environs. Wandering minstrels or court bards first recited it in verse and prose in palaces, inns and military encampments in France and elsewhere. No one knows who first told the tale but all its elements are well within the realm of possibility in view of the natural tendencies and talents of dogs.

Hercules was a familiar inmate of the royal palace in Paris when that city was a mere township compared to the capital of today, its streets mostly narrow, cobbled thoroughfares flanked by steep-roofed wood or stone dwellings. The biggest dog among the many canines in the palace, Hercules had a gentle disposition which made him popular with young and old alike, commoner or noble.

Hercules' master was the Chevalier Aubry de Montdidier, a gallant young knight who was one of the king's favorite guardsmen. The dog was a woolly pup when he was presented to Aubry by his father. He was promptly named Hercules because it was clear even then that he would be a big, powerful animal in maturity.

Aubry's mother had died some years previously and his father fell ill and died shortly after presenting his son with the pup. The dog and the orphaned knight became inseparable companions, at court and in Aubry's frequent hunting trips in the great forests girdling Paris.

Hercules, when fully grown, twice saved his master's life. On one occasion he dragged him from the Seine River when he was in danger of drowning and on another fought off a pack of wolves that might have overwhelmed the knight if the dog had not been with him.

This happy companionship might have lasted for many years

but for the Sieur de Macaire, a knight at the court who had anything but a friendly disposition. In a tournament held before the king and his court, Aubry and Macaire clashed on horseback and Aubry's deft spear sent his opponent rolling in the dust.

Macaire had no good sportsmanship in his makeup and thoughts of revenge mushroomed in his heart. After the tournament he never spoke to Aubry, who was not aware that Macaire was daily spying on his every move, awaiting a good opportunity to strike.

On a fine spring morning, de Montdidier, mounted on a spirited horse and armed with sword, lance and dagger, entered the forest of Bondis, accompanied by his faithful hound.

The trio were advancing at a leisurely pace through the trees when Hercules stopped suddenly and growled. Aubry reined in his mount and soon heard the sound of approaching hoofbeats. A knight in full armor on a black horse, lance in hand and sword on hip, materialized in the forest shadows and cantered toward them. His helmet did not cover his face and Aubry immediately recognized the newcomer as Macaire.

Hercules continued to growl menacingly but whatever suspicions beset Aubry were dispelled by Macaire's manner.

"This is indeed a pleasant surprise, Sieur Aubry," Macaire said with a friendly smile. "There should be good hunting today. Perhaps I may join you and we shall have two lances and two swords to bring down our quarry?"

Although somewhat surprised by this cordiality, Aubry replied, "Certes, you may do so, let us be friends from now on and forget that passage-at-arms, it was just play. I meant you no ill, next time you may well win."

Seeing the two men in amicable conversation, his master quite at ease, Hercules ceased his growling and bounded ahead as the two riders spurred their mounts deeper into the forest. Gradually Macaire let his horse fall behind that of Aubry. As the path grew narrower, he suddenly couched his spear, raked his horse into a forward lunge, and drove the spear deep into the back of Aubry, who was not wearing armor.

Aubry pitched to the ground with a groan and lay still. Dismounting, Macaire ascertained he was dead and dragged the body behind some bushes and threw it into a ditch. He began to cover it with earth and leaves but before he could finish the job Hercules was there. With a terrible howl the dog threw itself upon the body and began feverishly to lick the dead man's face. This gave Macaire time to remount and gallop away. He was jubilant. The killing had occurred deep in a vast forest and no human had seen the deed. As far as he was concerned the dog was of no importance, neither was the dead knight's horse. If the body was found the killing would probably be blamed on forest robbers who abounded in France at that time.

For two days and two nights, Hercules crouched at the side of the slain knight. No one heard his desperate howls. On the third morning hunger and thirst compelled him to leave the forest and he returned to the king's palace in Paris.

Servants fed him and puzzled over his haggard, unkempt appearance and irritable manner. Suddenly the dog ran upstairs to a room where knights were wont to assemble.

"Ha, Aubry must be back, Hercules is here," one of them said.

"Pardieu, that is correct and I wonder where Aubry has been hiding," said another.

The dog gazed around the big hall. Suddenly he sniffed the air, let out a roar, and bounded toward one of the cavaliers. It was Macaire. The knight, whose only arm at this moment was a poniard, shouted for help and other men pulled Hercules away. No one could understand why the dog, usually so gentle, had become so angry against one particular man. Macaire stated emphatically that he never had done anything likely to arouse the animal's ire.

Hercules fled the palace and resumed his vigil in the forest next to the body. Hunger again drove him back to the palace and once again he had to be restrained in an attack against Macaire. The suspicions of some of the noblemen had been aroused, however, and Hercules, on a long leash, led them and their horses to the scene of the crime in the forest.

The body was brought back to Paris for a Christian burial and the noblemen reported their discovery to the king. The king ordered all his cavaliers, hundreds of them, to assemble in one of the large halls in the palace. Then Hercules was let in. Ignoring all the other personages present, he made straight for Macaire, only to be pulled away for the third time.

The king was convinced by this that Macaire was involved in the crime. The king decided that the dog's behavior constituted a formal accusation just as though one of Aubry's kinsmen had accused Macaire in the royal presence. The monarch then ruled that a duel should take place between Macaire and the dog in which God would point to the vanquished as the liar.

The fight took place in a small arena in Paris in the presence of the king and the entire court. Macaire was given a heavy club and a shield but carried no body armor except a light helmet. Hercules was given a broad leather collar studded with nails as a partial bodily protection. An empty barrel was placed in the arena to which the dog could retreat if necessary.

When released by one of the umpires in the arena, Hercules hurtled toward Macaire, who was standing some twenty paces away, ready for combat. For several minutes the dog could not get in close. Macaire was a seasoned fighter and wielded his club and shield with skill. Repeatedly Hercules was kept at bay by the club, suffering a number of stiff blows. He was a crafty canine, however, and after a quick feint pierced his foe's defense and clamped his fangs on Macaire's throat. The knight fell to the ground howling for mercy.

The dog was dragged off and when the king entered the arena

the wounded man confessed the killing of Aubry in the forest. A few days later he was sentenced to death and quartered. His remains were dragged through the streets of Paris. Hercules lived on at the court, honored by all.

This story is known as "The Dog of Montargis," apparently as a result of a mural decoration that King Charles V of France ordered in 1371 for his castle at Montargis, some 200 miles south of Paris. The mural, depicting the famous duel, was painted on a wall above a fireplace, with an inscription reading:

The duel between a dog and a nobleman who had killed his master, made at Montargis under the reign of Charles V in 1371.

As a result of this inscription historians of the seventeenth and eighteenth centuries took the view that the duel had occurred in the year 1371 during the reign of Charles V. The drama occurred much earlier, probably in the eleventh century, according to deductions made by Fairfax Downey, American writer and authority on canine history. He writes in his book *Great Dog Stories of All Time:*

Strangely enough, an error of punctuation seems to be the reason for assigning the duel to 1371. . . . Obviously it was the painting that was done in 1371 and this did not signify that the fight occurred then. But the error stuck and later historians tell the story under the title "The Dog of Montargis." Even Montargis itself accepted the historical error and in its public garden there stands a statue illustrating the famous tale.

It is easy to understand why this story was popular during the Middle Ages. Not only is it a fine dog story with a knightly background, but the ordeal, the "Gottesurteil" (judgment of God) where a public trial is interpreted as the expression of God's will, is quite typical of that period.

One would think that with the beginning of the 19th century the story would have lost some of its appeal to the public. But just the opposite is true.

On June 18, 1814, the melodrama *The Dog of Montargis* opened at the Théâtre de la Gaîté in Paris. The play was a smash hit and continued to be played for some 20 years in the midst of political and military convulsions which included the downfall of Emperor Napoleon at Waterloo in 1815.

The author of the melodrama was an obscure Monsieur Pixerecourt. Well-trained canine performers were required for the title role. Dog stars in this play had to be real actors. They had to jump through a gate, ring a bell, obey numerous cues for barks and down the villain with suitable gusto in the climactic mock duel.

The play also was performed with success in London and elsewhere in Europe. Until the advent of the motion picture it undoubtedly was the most notable theatrical production starring dogs.

Some versions of the story say that a lovely court damsel caused Macaire's anger toward de Montdidier. Both men were courting her but she definitely favored Aubry, provoking murderous jealousy in her other suitor.

Another equally famous story is that of the wolfhound Gelert, this one stressing a dog's high sense of guardianship, his foe a wolf. Gelert lived in the twelfth century, the favorite dog of Prince Llewelyn an Iorwerth of Wales. The prince went hunting one day leaving Gelert behind in his castle to mount guard over his master's baby son. Returning from the hunt, the prince found the overturned cradle empty and splotched with blood. Blood also spattered the dog standing near the cradle. The prince believed Gelert had eaten his child and stabbed him to the heart. Almost immediately he heard a feeble cry and found the boy unharmed under the bed. Next to him lay the body of a giant wolf that had been killed by Gelert in protecting the child. A tablet next to a tree near Snowdon, Wales, notes that Gelert was reputedly buried there and recounts the story.

Such historical anecdotes and stories underscore a dog's ability to sense impending danger and give warning and its ability to remember a person or persons. The animal's supersensitive nose is probably the main factor, hearing and sight being secondary.

One of the greatest living authorities on animal psychology and behavior is the Italian writer Guglielmo Bonuzzi. Dogs will rarely attack another dog which has been injured or is blind or enfeebled by age, he states. In many cases dogs will instinctively aid another animal in distress. He cites among many instances one in which a dog on its own volition plunged into the Tiber River in Rome and rescued a drowning cat. On another occasion a dog spotted a mouse crouching in the middle of a Roman street in danger of death from a passing vehicle. The dog gently picked up the mouse and laid it down in a safe spot at the base of a building. The dog then departed on its own journeys. The mouse was totally blind, Bonuzzi was told by a passerby who witnessed the incident and had held the mouse in his hand for a brief moment after the rescue.

Some interesting comments on the various senses of dogs are contained in a booklet published by the U. S. Army entitled *Military Dog Training and Employment,* compiled by expert handlers. The booklet says in part:

Dogs so far surpass man in keenness of smell that it is difficult to imagine the nature of the smell sensations they receive. Just as it is probably impossible for a dog to imagine what colors are, so it is impossible for man to conceive the vast range of odors and delicate differences in chemical shading to which a dog is so sensitive. The dog's nose is ideally adapted for the detection of minute amounts of odorous particles. It is kept moist by a glandular secretion and is extremely sensitive to slight currents of air. On feeling such a current, a dog turns his head into the wind, clears his nostrils and sniffs.

A generous sample of the air passes into the nasal cavity and over the mucous membrane, which is richly supplied with finely subdivided endings of the olfactory nerves. The mucous membrane is supported on a complex bone structure. Its structure is such as to present maximum surface with a minimum obstruction to the circulation of air. In general, studies show that dogs can respond to odor traces of all known sorts, in dilutions far greater than can be detected by man. Furthermore, they can distinguish odors which to a human seem identical.

A dog's trailing ability depends upon certain traits in addition to his sense of smell. Almost any German Shepherd has a good enough sense of smell to become a good trailer, but it is only the exceptional dog that can be trained to follow slowly and carefully any trail his master sets him on, regardless of any diversion or olfactory complication he may encounter. Any Shepherd can trail a rabbit or a woodchuck. Only a few will, on command, follow the trail of a stranger leading through traffic, under snow, near a kennel full of dogs, or past a woodchuck hole.

Tests indicate that a dog's success in trailing depends primarily upon his accurate assessment of such factors as: earth odor from the compression of those spots stepped upon by his quarry; plant odor from the vegetation bruised or broken by his quarry; odor traces from shoes and shoe polish; odor traces from decaying animal or other organic matter; body odor specific to any particular person.

Visual clues are of slight assistance to him.

Tests have been conducted to prove that a dog hears sounds too faint to affect human ears. Also the dog hears sounds of higher pitch than can a human. In using a dog's sense of hearing to assist in training, you will find that voice inflection as well as the sound of actual words affects his understanding of oral commands. Some dogs appear to understand most accurately the feeling and wishes of the handler as they are conveyed by his voice. A word spoken in an encouraging tone will elate dogs; a cross word will depress them. If it is intended to use a dog at night or under any circumstances where he cannot see his handler, it is important to train him to respond to a number of oral commands.

A most striking difference between the retina of a dog's eye and that of a human is that the dog's retina lacks a fovea centralis, which is a small rodless area of the retina that affords acute vision.

When a man focuses his eyes upon any object, the light reflected from that object is thrown upon the fovea centralis. He can see many other objects besides that one, but he sees them indistinctly. This can be tested readily enough by focusing the eyes upon any word on this printed page and then trying to see how many other words can be read without moving the eyes. The words reflected upon the nonfoveal portions of the retina are poorly defined. Since a dog lacks a fovea centralis, one may expect that even an object upon which he focuses is seen less clearly than it would be by humans.

Perception of movement is a type of visual stimulation to which dogs seem very sensitive. If an object is moved ever so slightly, most dogs will detect it and respond to the movement. Dogs make little use of their eyes in learning except for their perception of movements.

Experimental evidence supports the opinion that to dogs the world looks like a black and white photograph.

As regards intelligence, the booklet says, "the dog is far inferior to man, but probably superior to any other animal below the primates," and adds:

A dog can be taught to respond appropriately to an extremely large number of spoken words. No one knows the limit of his vocabulary. Under ordinary working conditions, only about 20 words are needed, but some dogs have been known to master responses to well over 100 oral commands.

How a dog can use these senses in crime detection is underscored in a dramatic story contained in the book *Man's Best Friend*, a history of dogs past and present by the British author A. H. Trapman. According to the author there can be little question that it actually occurred although such details as names of persons, the type of dog involved and the exact dates to the month and year cannot be ascertained. The story is reminiscent of the feat of Hercules but in a totally different setting.

In the late 1600's an English gentleman of some means had his country home on the Kentish shore of the Thames, Trapman says. Strolling on his lawn one summer's day he perceived a dog swimming toward the shore. The animal obviously was coming from a mud flat in the river, a dreary expanse of land covered by rank grass. Landing on the shore, the animal disappeared among some nearby trees where the small cottage of a farmer was located.

About a half hour later the country squire noticed that the dog swam back to the island and disappeared in the grass. At first the man's interest was not especially aroused. But when the dog repeated his action the following day and for several days thereafter, his curiosity sharpened and he decided to investigate. He questioned the farmer and the latter informed him that the dog had been doing this for several weeks. The dog was not known to the farmer when he first appeared in his garden, obviously desiring food. The dog was a friendly animal and the farmer had fed him the first time and had continued to do so in ensuing days. The dog always ate his food and then returned to the island regardless of the weather.

The gentleman decided that he also would become friends with the strange dog and, following the example of the farmer, began to feed him when he came ashore. He and the dog became great friends and since the farmer was old and poor the squire soon assumed the entire task of feeding the animal.

At first the squire presumed that the visitor belonged to some fisherman residing in a shanty on the island or using it as a base for his daily labors. Learning, however, that it was totally uninhabited, he decided to investigate that area.

He followed the swimming dog to the island in a rowboat one day and once both were on land strode after the animal. At some distance inland behind a low hummock the dog stopped suddenly beside a mound of earth, and lay down with his head between his forepaws, his eyes doleful and beseeching.

Arriving at the spot, the squire noted that the mound had a somewhat artificial appearance, as if created by a shovel or pickax. He kicked some of the earth away and his puzzlement soon vanished.

The mound was a grave. Inside was the decomposing body of a man. His battered skull clearly indicated that he had been killed by the blows of a heavy club or a rock. The remnants of his clothing indicated that he was a poor man, possibly a fisherman or a Thames River bargeman. Evidently the criminal or criminals had hastily buried him.

Leaving the dog to his faithful vigil, the squire returned to his home and ordered servants to go to the island and bring the body back to the mainland for burial. A close study of the remains before burial provided no clue as to the man's identity or where he came from.

The gentleman then formally adopted the dog and the animal was comfortably kenneled on his grounds. From then on, the dog did not return to the island but almost daily visited the nearby grave of the man who undoubtedly had been his former master.

Many months after the discovery of the body the squire traveled to London to make some purchases and visit some friends. The dog, by now a devoted companion, accompanied him. When the time came to return to the country seat, the squire, his dog by his side, went down to a wharf near the Tower of London where boatmen were for hire. He was driving a bargain with one for the homeward trip when another boatman pulled in and alighted on the wharf.

He had barely done so when the dog, hackles bristling, attacked him fiercely, inflicting several wounds on the man's legs. The man thoroughly frightened, pleaded that the dog be held back, which the squire did. The squire, however, was convinced that the man had something to do with the murder on the mud flat. Threatening him with a fresh attack by the infuriated dog, the squire drew a confession from the man that he had killed and robbed the dog's master. Then he had buried him. The bargeman was seized and jailed. The squire and his dog returned to the country estate but both were present in London when the culprit was publicly hanged.

The area where the man was murdered is still called today Island of the Dogs. Many residents in this part of England feel, however, that it should really be called Island of the Dog, since its name obviously was adopted as a result of this episode. It had no particular name before the incident.

How a dog tracked a lawbreaker in Germany is lucidly portrayed with text and map in a book published recently in Germany, written by Kurt Koenig. It is entiteld *Mein Freund Hussan auf Gefährlicher Fahrte* (My Friend Hussan on Dangerous Missions). The book is mainly about the author's favorite Alsatian, Hussan, and the manner in which he aided police, particularly in coping with smugglers in mountain terrain. In one chapter, not dealing with Hussan, the author describes an incident that occurred in the German countryside about 50 years ago. The incident developed as follows:

Shortly before 2 A.M one day a farmer left the village of Y where he had been visiting relatives and proceeded on foot toward the nearby village of X, where he lived. He was following a country road that at one point was bisected by a main thoroughfare. The country road ribboned through fairly open farmland but near the village of X it cut through a rather dense forest. After crossing a footbridge spanning a small stream, the farmer was suddenly attacked by a man lurking in the shrubbery. He was knocked down and the attacker fled with his pocketbook, containing money, various papers he had on his person and a gold wedding ring.

The victim, though stunned, was not seriously hurt, and almost immediately he got up and hurried to X village where he reported the assault to the police. Two constables accom-

An Alsatian of the Metropolitan Police of London is led out of one of the dog division's special radio cars. Part of the grill work enclosing the section of the car in which a dog or dogs are placed is visible.

A London police dog and his handler in a routine building patrol. Regular police handlers wear a special flat cap with visor as seen in this picture.

Police of Freeport, Long Island, nail a "fugitive" in a realistic night training operation. Patrolman Gary Steinberg is holding Casper, who is growling and prepared to obey any order from his handler.

Police Chief Edward Dixon and men and dogs of the Freeport K-9 division. Shortly after this picture was taken, it was decided that four dogs would be adequate, and Bruno, the alert canine at the right, was "honorably discharged." His then handler adopted him as a pet.

Casper is readied for an attack by Steinberg in a Freeport training demonstration.

One of the Freeport dogs being prepared for a tracking test with long leash.

Freeport dogs in general-attack agitation on the training ground. In this phase dogs are held carefully on leash since the "criminal" is not protected by padded apparel.

A typical police dog training area enclosing various types of obstacles.

Police dog negotiates a ladder in training.

A dog of the Baltimore, Maryland, K-9 division in an all-out attack against a policeman in a fully padded protective suit. Dog will promptly release his hold upon command of his handler stationed nearby.

panied him back to the scene as dawn was breaking and searched the area but could find no clues. They decided to call in the dog of a local friend, an Alsatian male, known to be a good tracker. On various occasions the dog had helped the police find lost children.

Accompanied by his master, the dog was brought on the scene at about 6 A.M. After circling awhile, the canine nosed down on what he seemed to feel was a good trail at point No. 1 on the map. Straining at the leash held by his master, he headed for the banks of the stream. Although he was following what is termed a cold trail in view of the time elapsed since the robber had struck, the dog obviously was having no trouble following it.

At No. 2 the dog and his master, the two policemen and the farmer crossed the stream, the dog picking up the trail unhesitatingly on the other side. Suddenly the dog stopped at 3 and sniffed carefully in a patch of deep grass. His master knew that he was looking for something. He was proven correct when the four-footed hunter found a pocketbook in the verdure. The farmer immediately identified the find as his. It was empty, as was to be expected.

Receiving a friendly pat from his master, the dog continued the chase. At 4 and 5 he hesitated for some time. The trail was confusing him—as was established later. Another farmer had cut across the field in this area two hours prior to 2 A.M. when the attack occurred. By now, nevertheless, the men were fairly certain that the dog was hot on the right trail.

No. 6 on the map was a critical point. Here the fugitive could have decided to leave the fields and taken several directions along either the country road or the main thoroughfare. The Alsatian was not long in trouble and plowed ahead toward the forest beyond the road, indicating the fugitive had decided not to use any roads. At 7 on entering the forest the dog was temporarily baffled again by some change in terrain but got on the scent again and plunged deeper into the woods. At 8 he picked up another object—a small manila envelope. It was empty but was identified by the victim as his. It had contained the stolen papers.

The dog now swung back and at 9 and 10 his actions revealed that the thief had again stepped on the country road, moved to the intersection of the roads, and decided to reenter the field he had originally traversed. Moving across the field toward 11, the animal was again briefly bothered by the cross-scent he had met at 4 and 5. At 11 he changed direction again, heading straight across the main highway. It was discovered later that at this point the fugitive had hidden briefly in some bushes, having perceived that policemen had arrived on the scene of the robbery and were searching the immediate vicinity. At 12 there was another change of direction and at 13 the dog was again baffled fleetingly and lost some minutes in picking up the original trail. This confusion was caused by the trail of yet another farmer who, at 5 A.M., had crossed this field to gain the main highway. At 14 the dog again crossed the country road, moving surely, re-entered the forest and came to a halt at the door of a small barn, growling angrily.

Here, at 15, the chase ended after having covered some 4 to 5 miles. The fugitive was inside the barn. He confessed after a brief questioning and confrontation with the pocketbook and manila envelope picked up by the dog. The police also found the lost papers and currency on his person, which left no doubt in their minds that this was the culprit. He was placed under arrest and given a fairly stiff jail sentence.

Obviously, the robber never expected a dog on his trail. But for the Alsatian he might never have been caught. The man was a drifter and planned to leave the barn that day and head for other points. There was no person who could identify him as the bandit. His victim did not know what he looked like. If he had foreseen the possibility that a dog would be used, he could have waded through the stream for a considerable distance. This maneuver can seriously hinder dog tracking. It is questionable that the police by themselves would ever have found the pocketbook and the envelope. Without the Alsatian hot on the trail it might well have been another case of a lawbreaker getting away with it—another unsolved crime on police blotters.

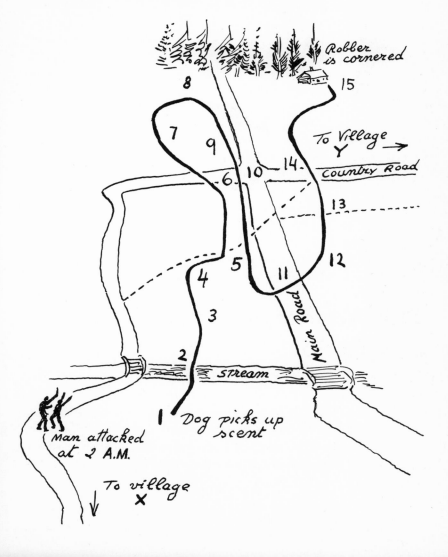

ORBAAN

Two dogs of black Saint Hubert's breed
Unmatch'd for courage, breath and speed
Fast on his flying traces came. . . .
        —Sɪʀ Wᴀʟᴛᴇʀ Sᴄᴏᴛᴛ, *Lady of the Lake.*

4

The Adventures of
Edwin Richardson

THE last fight of Binks was swift and terrible.

A David against a Goliath, he waged it alone in his master's house when darkness blanketed the English countryside. No friendly human ears heard his frenzied barks or his last whimper. He was not a trained police dog but his final exploit merits an accolade in any police K-9 annals. He provided the law with a startling and shocking clue after he was dead.

Binks was a lively, intelligent, curly-haired Airedale owned by Lieut. Col. Edwin de Hautenville Richardson, one of Britain's most famous dog trainers and an outstanding pioneer in dog-man law enforcement.

Richardson, who gained note for his work with dogs at the turn of the century and during World War I years, frequently sold one or more of his trained canines of various types to interested buyers for guard duty or as hunting companions.

In the year 1906 an Englishman whose home was in a rather isolated area contacted Richardson and told him that he and his wife wanted to purchase a good guard dog.

"There have been a series of robberies in our vicinity and we both fear that our house may be the next," he told Richardson.

"I have one for you, I believe, a really good fellow, alert and afraid of neither man nor devil," Richardson replied.

Richardson, a spare man of medium height with keen blue eyes and sandy hair, then led his visitor to the yard where his dogs were kept. He pointed to Binks and declared this was the dog he had in mind. While admitting that Binks was a fine specimen of its breed, the would-be purchaser expressed some dissatisfaction. Although fully grown, Binks was far from impressive physically. Richardson assured his visitor, however, that any housebreaker would have a rough time if this Airedale was around, and the sale was concluded. With a final pat on the head from Edwin, Binks left with his new master and headed on leash for the railway station and his new home, located in central England. That was the last time Richardson saw the dog. Several weeks elapsed before the vendor learned what happened to Binks. A constable who knew Richardson and had been at the scene phoned him the details shortly after the police wound up the case.

The case, a rather extraordinary one in the annals of crime, developed as follows:

A few weeks after the purchase of Binks, his new owners left their home for a day's outing with friends. The Airedale remained behind on guard in the house where all windows and doors had been shut. No servants were in the building. Binks had been left on guard in this manner on several previous occasions for varying lengths of time, with adequate food and water available. The dog had been well trained by Richardson, liked his new home and owners, and took such lonely vigils in his stride.

Husband and wife returned to the house late in the evening when night had fallen. When they entered the front door and turned on the lights everything seemed in order, except for the fact that some of the carpets were rumpled. Uneasiness gripped both man and woman almost immediately. There was no welcoming bark, no happy Binks rushing toward them. Only ominous silence. They soon perceived that something had happened in their absence.

A rear window had been broken and opened. Obviously a burglar had entered and possibly was still around. The man immediately phoned the local police.

Then they found Binks. He was stretched out lifeless on a carpet in one of the rooms on the main floor. One side of his head was blood-spattered and flecks of gore spotted the rug. Both decided not to touch the dog until the police came.

When a constable arrived on the scene the owner had some deprecatory words for his late guard dog, not unjustified in view of the evidence on hand. Apparently, he told the policeman, the dog had not put up much of a fight, just let himself be killed. After a rapid survey of the building to ascertain whether an intruder was still present, which proved negative, the constable entered the room where the dog lay and bent down to examine the wound.

"Looks as if he had been belted by a lead pipe or some type of club," the policeman said. "Poor blighter, his skull's fair cracked open—a really smashing blow."

The policeman then lifted the dog's head off the carpet to see whether any other wounds had been inflicted in the cranial area. No other wounds were visible, but as he did so the dog's jaws opened and something fell to the ground.

"Blimey, wot's this mess?" the constable grunted.

The two onlookers gasped.

It was a man's thumb—a big thumb, virtually all of it, bloody stump at one end, grimy nail at the other.

Binks had fought; he had not failed to do his bit.

It did not take the police long to run down a man whose thumb had been recently severed. An alarm was immediately sent out, followed by a tip from a druggist in a nearby town that he had hurriedly bandaged the hand of a man who claimed he had lost his thumb in an accident. The following day the police cornered a suspect, a hulking man with a bloody bandage around his right hand. He first claimed that he had been injured in an accident, but when the policemen unwrapped the thumb the man broke down. He confessed that he killed the dog and was the perpetrator of various other burglaries which had plagued the region.

The burglar told police that the dog had attacked him almost immediately when he had entered the house. Deciding to kill the dog, he aimed a sweeping blow at his head with a lead pipe held in his right hand. The dog ducked and lunged at the lowered hand and with a violent snap bit off most of his thumb. Retaining his grip on his weapon in spite of the injury, he then delivered a second and lethal blow. Frightened and in sharp pain, he hurriedly stanched his wound with a handkerchief and fled, all thoughts of looting at an end. He was duly given a stiff jail sentence.

Saddened by the loss of their pet, Binks' owners buried him near their home. On his grave they placed a small plaque bearing the words: *Here lies Binks, a good dog, stout friend to the end.*

Shortly after the burial they bought another dog from Richardson. It was an Airedale named Billy. It was promptly rechristened Binks.

Binks' case is cited by Richardson in his authoritative and engrossing book *Forty Years with Dogs* which recounts his experiences in Britain and various other countries, for his work carried him far and wide.

A well-educated man with a distinguished military ancestry, Richardson, following a youthful army career, devoted virtually all of his life to the training of dogs for various types of work. One of his most notable achievements involved the organization of large dog units for the British armed forces in World War I. These animals distinguished themselves in finding wounded men, carrying messages over dangerous and difficult battle terrain and acting as sentries in the war zones, principally on the Western Front.

Besides the volume cited above, he wrote several other books about his experiences with dogs, one of them specifically dealing with law enforcement and the other with war dogs. They all included valuable information on training and are still considered authoritative guideposts in this domain long after the death of the author from natural causes.

In the late 1800's and in the early years of this century—when Richardson was most active—the creation of official police K-9 units as we know them today was still a thing of the future in Britain and in virtually all other countries. Germany and also Belgium were showing the way impressively with widespread use of officially enrolled police dogs, relying principally on the newly bred German shepherd. The trend, however, only gained real momentum in other countries after World War I.

Nonetheless, the British police and the greater part of the public were fully aware of the value of dogs in law enforcement work. The policemen, notably rural constables, had their own canine pets as companions and on many occasions found them useful as aides in running down lawbreakers or finding missing persons.

Richardson was never officially enrolled in the police but the authorities frequently sought his aid in baffling cases where the help of a skilled handler and highly trained canines was essential. As a result, Richardson was time and again involved in exciting and arduous operations, he and his dog or dogs unofficial "coppers."

To what curious places I have been led in this pursuit of criminals! [he wrote]. I have been awakened by a furious ringing of the telephone at my bedside in the middle watches of the night with an urgent summons. The clear, matter of fact, but nonetheless serious voice of the police superintendent with explanatory information and directions for the journey. Then a motor drive at breakneck speed, through silent villages and along darkened country roads. The arrival at some strange spot with a silent figure stretched out, weeping women and the quiet forms of the policemen, moving about and controlling all.

A bloodhound or a pair of these dogs were his favorite aides in tracking people, as they had been of old in England and in other countries. Many of his accounts evoke the adventures of Conan Doyle's immortal Sherlock Holmes and the author and his fictional sleuth were much in the public mind at that time; lonely moors and mountain glens, elusive criminal fugitives, some of them murderers, bloodhounds baying in sunlight, moonlight, rain or fog, hot on the trail, tugging at their leashes, Richardson hard-pressed to keep up with their relentless pace.

There are some striking photographs in his books. Many of them were taken by his wife, Blanche, who was an enthusiastic and able helpmate to Richardson throughout his career.

One of them could portray Holmes himself.* It shows Richardson striding across a lonely, flat field on a gray day, his lean face shadowed by the turned-down brim of his soft, tweed hat, a rumpled mackintosh over his casual winter suit, lower legs encased in leggings, his feet in sturdy walking shoes. A big bloodhound, with furrowed brow, tail erect, head low, is straining at the leash held in Richardson's left hand. The caption merely says *Bloodhound tracking*, leaving it to the reader's imagination whether the pair are off on a real hunt or merely on a jaunt.

On some occasions the police were not wholly cooperative, eager to reap the credit of solving a case themselves and not very keen on furnishing Richardson with clues.

However, this churlish attitude was not very often in evidence and as a rule I found them very good fellows. It must be understood that every possible help should be given to the handler of hounds in the matter of where the fugitive was last seen, irrespective of where the crime actually took place. Any article being found belonging to a fugitive should be reported as every little item of news of this nature is a help in showing where the scent lies strongest and most recently.

Some dogs are more intelligent than others, increasing the effective use of such natural characteristics as acute scent and hearing. One of Richardson's favorite bloodhounds was named Solferino, after a battle in which the French defeated the Aus-

---

* In Conan Doyle's famous story "The Sign of Four," a London mutt—a particularly intelligent dog—is of some help to Holmes during his efforts to solve the case. One of the most famous fictional dogs of all time was created by Doyle in another Holmes story, "The Hound of the Baskervilles," but this was a dog used for murderous purposes. Aside from "The Sign of Four," I do not believe the case of a dog helping the great detective occurs again in the stories. I cannot vouch for this, however.

trians in 1859. The dog was familiarly known as "Solly" or "Old Solly."

He was not quite purebred, but very nearly so, and was a "wonderful animal" since he combined an unusual amount of general intelligence with excellent nose talent.

I do not consider bloodhounds particularly intelligent in a wide sense, although they are very dignified fine fellows and look very wise, but they are hounds first and the other qualities follow after. Solly, however, had a sense of humor and was a great wag. He was self-willed and when on the trail would stop for nothing. I used him on a long lead and many a good run he gave me. I do not think I ever saw him tired. I believe he could have worked day and night for a week without fatigue so strong was he.

Solly was a "very engaging" animal of excellent hunting stock and had much more natural brainpower than the average hound, whose intelligence "to a great extent is concentrated in its nose and nowhere else." He was particularly responsive to recasting, the operation in which a dog has to pick up a scent which has been lost entirely or becomes so meager that the tracking animal is at a loss.

In view of Solly's outstanding talents, Richardson was able on numerous occasions to shatter the fallacy that if a person or animal passed through a stream this would completely throw a dog off the trail.

When checked at the water's edge Solly plunged in and immediately sought the other side. Here he would himself commence casting about and when I joined him was quick to follow my instructions as to the direction in which it seemed best to look for the continuation of the trail. In bloodhound trailing the hound and his handler must work together and must be one in intention. The latter should keep his eyes open for any evidences of footmarks or broken bushes or twigs which might point the way of the fugitive, and the hound thus can be aided on his way. [This advice holds good for trailing with any type of dog. Ed.]

Richardson and his dogs had their share of successes and failures. Most setbacks were due to a frequently occurring factor which often nullifies the dog's trailing skill. For one reason or another, generally a belated notice that canine help is wanted, the dog or dogs and their handler arrive too late in the area where there is a telltale scent. The scent which should be picked up has virtually vanished, frequently because of elapsed hours and changing weather conditions or the fact that many persons have tramped about on the critical terrain. The odds against even the most superb dog are virtually insuperable when confronted with such difficulties—the animal is stymied and so is his handler.

The ticklish factor of elapsed time confronted Edwin and his dogs in one of the most dramatic pursuits in his career, one in which Solly played an outstanding part.

Evening shadows were merging into darkness and rain was falling dismally when the phone jangled in the modest but comfortable home of the Richardsons, then residing in Surrey. Richardson, who was just sitting down to dinner with his wife, rose and answered the call. After a brief exchange of words he hung up the receiver and informed his wife that he would have to leave immediately on a police case. His wife, accustomed to such emergencies, packed a small bag with sandwiches, some dog food, various toiletries and spare socks, shirts and underclothing. Hurriedly finishing some of the food on the table, Richardson clapped a warm hat on his head, donned his mackintosh, selected a stout cane and informed Blanche quickly of what was afoot. Then he kissed her goodbye, promised to phone back as soon as possible, and opening the front door, headed for the nearby kennels. As Richardson recalled:

The summons had come from far in the north. By going straight off as I was, I caught the night mail [train] with the bloodhounds and arrived at a mining village on the east coast of Scotland.

Dawn was breaking and cold mists were circling around a bleak little cottage where lay the pathetic figure of a child—a little lad foully done to death by some unknown individual. Furious indignation gripped me at the dreadful sight.

Fortunately some definite marks had been left in the soft mud near the place and by comparing them with the footgear of those persons about the place it was possible to see that they did not correspond and must be the tracks of some stranger. Thirty-six hours had now elapsed since the murder had been discovered, but the air had been damp and foggy and the scent of the murderer had gradually fallen to the ground, where it had lain more or less undisturbed as, owing to the fog, not many people had passed that way.

Nevertheless, the chase was stern and very difficult. I had my good Solly and one other, a very excellent bitch who started on the trail well. The fugitive had followed the main road on which many feet had trodden. But he had, however, evidently from fear of recognition, made detours from the road on the country terrain on each side, taking refuge behind bushes and trees. In this way when we lost the trail on the highway we were able to pick it up further on by casting more widely on each side. I shall never forget that hunt! For several hours we never stopped working and at last we approached a fork in the road, one side of which led to a town and the other to the railway station.

Without hesitation the hounds went straight up the road to the station. Inquiries down the line had, of course, already been made by the police but this steady tracking work was in itself so convincing that further urgent messages were immediately sent to all R.R. stations with the result that the man who ultimately proved to be the murderer was arrested and brought to justice.*

---

* In many accounts Richardson does not give exact place names or dates but there is no question about the authenticity of his stories.

Although nothing is mentioned in the book regarding other developments, Edwin and his two dogs, their work done, presumably returned that same day by train to Surrey and a well-earned rest.

On another occasion elsewhere in England three "gentlemen of the underworld" were casting longing glances at a house owned by a wealthy couple named Fortescue. The trio decided to leave nothing to chance and carefully "cased the joint." Learning by various means that the house would be vacant on a certain night—the owner off on a business trip, the wife and two children at the theater, and the maid visiting a friend—the three Raffles decided the moment opportune to make a haul. What they did not know was that on the same day he left for his business trip Mr. Fortescue had transacted some urgent business with Richardson, who resided nearby. This involved immediate delivery to the house of a female Airedale named Bess. The females of this breed are smaller than the males and therefore less impressive but they make excellent watchdogs.

Bess was left behind when the other inmates of the house departed and the windows and doors closed. Lights were left on in a part of the ground floor. Everything was quiet in the building for several hours but Bess was on the alert. Shortly before eleven there was a tinkle of glass and three shadows entered the building through a window.

Mrs. Fortescue and her children returned from the theater shortly after eleven. They could hear the dog barking, but this did not make Mrs. Fortescue uneasy since this might just be canine pleasure over their return. What the tenants saw when they opened the front door is best described in Richardson's own words:

The little bitch was flying round and round the three burglars, biting here and biting there till in very mercy she had to be requested by her mistress to desist. The burglars, unprepared for such an eventuality, were thoroughly submissive. The local constable did the rest.

In another guard dog incident, Richardson and his helpers failed to take a vital factor into account, and a rather hilarious situation ensued reminiscent of early Keystone movie comedies.

The home of a Mr. and Mrs. Henry Jones had been burgled during the night and on the following morning Mrs. Jones phoned Richardson. She wanted a dog in the house immediately, that very day, because her husband would be away on business till late that night. Richardson told her he had a fine male Airedale named Jock which he could sell her and that one of his men would deliver the animal to her house immediately.

This was done, but one point was overlooked. The animal had not been given a chance to get acquainted with either master or mistress. A carefully trained guard animal, he thought it was his duty to protect the premises against any strangers.

Late that night the phone jangled in Richardson's house and he rose sleepily from his bed. At the other end was Mr. Jones, obviously in high dudgeon.

"Look here, Mr. Richardson, this is a fine state of affairs, I am calling you from the outside," he shouted. "I don't dare go into my own house. That dog almost got me when I opened the door. My wife is upstairs, wringing her hands, terribly frightened. Please do something fast."

Richardson got dressed and hurried over. The dog was soon quieted and made to realize that he had a new master and mistress. The dog had not harmed the woman in any way but had vigilantly prevented her from descending the stairs and obtaining help. There was no telephone upstairs and there were no nearby neighbors to whom she could shout. All attempts to change the Airedale's viewpoint with some candy and cookies she had in her room and such words as "dear doggy, good doggy" were futile.

Throughout history the British Isles have had their full quota of poachers of all types, some of them hard-bitten individuals prone to violent reactions if someone interfered with their activities.

There was a gang of them, tough customers all, operating in a part of Scotland where Edwin and Blanche Richardson were residing shortly after their marriage in 1894. The property around the Richardson cottage included some well-stocked trout ponds. These poachers specialized in illicit fish catching. They and Richardson became involved in an episode which had uproarious overtones.

At that time Richardson's reputation as a trainer of police and guard dogs was limited generally to friends and local neighbors and the fact that he had some very fine canine specimens on his grounds was either unknown to poachers or viewed as no threat to their nocturnal activities.

On a moonlit night Richardson perceived, through a window, mysterious forms moving about the trout ponds. He left the house and soon ascertained that a gang of fish poachers numbering about ten men was raiding one of the ponds with dragnets.

A courageous man in spite of his slight build, Edwin approached the men and shouted to them to get out. This was a bold move since his house had no telephone and was at some distance from the dwellings of neighbors.

Several of the men laughed out loud at the sight of the solitary challenger and one of them, apparently the leader, a big man with massive neck and shoulders, shouted back:

"Knock it off, guv'nor, knock it off, go back to the house and get some sleep, that will be healthy for you."

They were quite polite, Richardson recalled, but obviously were very determined men who would not easily cease their thievery.

"Very well, gentlemen, I fear I shall have to resort to strong measures, as I do not see why I should lose all my trout," Edwin replied.

The poachers merely laughed and went on with their work as Richardson turned on his heel and marched back to the house—and his kennels. There he released four Newfoundland dogs, all in prime condition, and headed back for the ponds.

An ominous sound suddenly re-echoed across the tree-speckled fields illuminated by a full moon—a sound lawbreakers of any type find disturbing.

"The dogs were surprised at this unwonted release at dead of night," Richardson recalled with a chuckle. "With joyful voices raised the dogs followed me toward the ponds and the moon shone down on four jet black dogs of gigantic size bursting through the trees.

"A few words of direction were sufficient and round those ponds one saw the most exciting chase which could be imagined. Round and round the ruffians ran trying to save their nets and themselves, but to no purpose. Very soon the one idea for them was to get away at all costs, which they eventually did, leaving all their tackle behind. This I handed over to the police the next day."

Frequently Richardson and his dogs were called in on "missing persons" cases. One of the most interesting occurred shortly after the trout pond incident but it had a tragic finale.

Police asked for Richardson's help at the request of a forester who lived in a small cottage on the edge of a large wood in eastern Scotland. He said he was uneasy about the fate of his old grandmother who lived in the cottage. Two days earlier the woman, who was very frail and somewhat feebleminded, had left the building and he at first believed she had headed for Glasgow. This city was nearby and she had friends there. She had done this before but invariably had returned to the cottage on the same day. The forester had contacted people in Glasgow whom she knew but none could provide him with any information. They had not seen her at all.

Richardson arrived on the scene with the trusty Solly and another bloodhound, not overly optimistic about the situation since 48 hours already had elapsed.

Edwin had the two hounds sniff the main door of the cottage and the path leading from it in the general direction of a nearby railway station, which the forester believed his "granny" had headed for.

Suddenly Solly gave "a most determined lead to the left" and took a line up the hill in quite an opposite direction from the nearby village and its railway station.

I followed and soon saw a tiny piece of dress fluttering on a bramble bush which proved to be of the same pattern as that which the old lady was wearing. Solly went on fairly steadily after this but once or twice I had to help him by recasting him further back and letting him pick up once more. After a time he gave tongue where the wood was enclosed and the ground rather swampy. Evidently in the still weather we had been having the body scent had lain near the ground almost without evaporating and dispersing. It was true that the old woman had wandered that way for Solly led us higher and higher until, with a despairing howl, he ended on the shore of a dark, evil-looking mountain tarn [lake].

Richardson and the police soon found the old lady but she was dead. Her body was lying in the water at the base of a cliff. In her wanderings she had evidently fallen over the cliff during the night and drowned.

Richardson admitted that there was nothing very sensational about this case. However, to a handler of hounds it was a most interesting assignment since the dogs, notably Solly, worked so conscientiously and with such consummate skill.

It is believed that bloodhounds were first introduced in the British Isles when William the Conqueror invaded the Saxon realm in 1066 and overwhelmed King Harold at the Battle of Hastings.

There were two types widely in use in France at that time. According to a British authority, Morrell Mackenzie, one was known as the White St. Hubert* which was the precursor of the dog known in Britain as the Southern Hound. Soon a somewhat different type of dog developed from this strain, known as the Otter Hound, another dog in the old British breed grouping. The other bloodhound known as the Black St. Hubert was a black and tan animal. Both the black and white animals were almost certainly brought over the Channel in William's fleet. The Black St. Hubert evolved ultimately into the bloodhound.

"The bloodhound seems to have altered very little from the original Black St. Hubert, which became extinct in the early part of the nineteenth century," Mackenzie says.

Robert the Bruce and Wallace, the Scottish heroes, were "certainly in danger on many occasions from the Sleuth Hound," the name loosely applied to this St. Hubert breed at the time, Mackenzie notes.

It was regularly used in the pursuit of fugitives, thieves, murderers, escaped serfs and the like. The type of dogs which hunted slaves in *Uncle Tom's Cabin* were not the same type of canine. This dog probably was a cross between a Cuban mastiff and a Great Dane. The real bloodhound of Europe was not introduced into the United States until 1888.

---

* Patron saint of the hunt. He was a great hunter and dog fancier but gave up hunting and turned to saintly ways after assertedly seeing a golden crucifix between the antlers of a stag which appeared before him in a forest.

Southern slaveowners in this country actually used foxhounds or mongrel dogs having a foxhound strain in them and somewhat resembling the true bloodhounds. Knowing about the real strain in Europe and fully aware of the ominous connotation in the name, they assiduously spread the news that real bloodhounds were available to intensify the fears of the Negroes, who were warned that these were the most infallible tracking dogs in the world.

Their dogs were savage beasts, especially one type known as the "Cuban bloodhound," a dog which was part mastiff, having none of the gentler strains of the purebred animal. The hounds of the slaveowners were kept and hunted in packs. A dog is always much more excited and determined when running with a number of others and will then do many things which in an ordinary way it would not attempt by itself.

There is a misconception that the name bloodhound means that the animal follows a blood trail, that it must sniff blood to be effective. This is not so—it just has exceptional scenting powers applicable to all kinds of odors. The name signifies that it is a "blooded hound" of a special breed.

A rather graphic description of bloodhounds was penned by a Dr. Caius, a sixteenth-century English authority on dogs, who lived in the reign of Queen Elizabeth. Dr. Caius discussed its capabilities as a hunting dog and seemed to hold the view that a blood smell was a vital guide to the dogs. He wrote:

The greater sort which serve to hunt, having lippes of great size and eares of no small length, do not only chase the beast whilst it liveth, but being dead also by any maner of casualtie, make recourse to the place where it lyeth, having on this point an assured infallible guyde, namely, the scent and savour of the blood sprinckled heyre and there upon the ground . . . these dogges with no less facilitie and easiness their aviditie and greedinesse can disclose and betray the same by smelling, applying to their pursute agilitie and nimblenesse without tediousness, for which consideration of a singal specialitie they deserve to be called Sanguinarrii, or Bloodhounds.

Caius also had some complimentary remarks regarding this breed's ability to hunt man, words actually applicable to dogs in general.

Creepe they never so farre into the thickest thronge, they will finde him out notwithstanding he lye hidden in wylde woods, in close and overgrowen groves and lurcke in hollow holes apte to harbour such ungracious guestes.

The impression has prevailed and probably will continue to prevail that bloodhounds are dangerous animals, prone to attack and destroy. This is entirely erroneous. The real bloodhound is basically a gentle animal more likely to give a human quarry, once found, a friendly tail wag than launch any form of attack.

Probably at no time in history has lawlessness of all types gained such scope and variety as it did during the Middle Ages in Europe. England, France and other countries were in constant tumult, torn by wars and feuds between robber barons and other ruthless nobles. Large areas were lightly populated, carpeted with trackless forests, the roads few and lonely. Woe to those who traveled far from castle or town singly or with companions unskilled in the use of arms. Throughout those troubled centuries dogs of all types proved invaluable "alarm bells" and very helpful friends to their masters when a fight developed.

In many respects the conditions prevailing in those days were exceptionally good for dogs on a manhunt. The roads, where they existed, were of a rough surface, favorable to retention of scent. A human scent trail on moor or other open terrain and in the forests was usually not apt to be mixed with other human smells. Personal cleanliness was not deemed next to godliness by any means. Practically everyone, even the high and mighty, had a nostril-filling body odor.

The bloodhounds used during the Elizabethan era and in prior centuries were savage animals, trained to attack, most historians believe. Aside from the chase they unquestionably were the preferred tracking animal in any manhunt in England, Scotland, Ireland and on the Continent.

A striking account of the perils of daily life in ancient times and how bloodhounds helped break up a canny gang of desperadoes is penned by Richardson in the chapter on police dogs in his book *Forty Years with Dogs*. Although his description deals with England and Scotland in the 1500's it could apply to almost any European country in that century or those preceding it.

Life in the outlying parts of England and in Scotland was a parlous affair. The husbandman kept his dirk close at hand and the mother clasped her babe in nervous embrace even when they slept. At any moment a howling war-cry of warning might rouse them to throbbing terror, a glance without the dwelling would reveal the beacons blazing red on the mountain tops against the darksome midnight sky.

The great bell on the castle tower would peal forth, calling, calling, calling—the men to battle, and the women and their children, the flocks and the herds to safety. The great door is open and through the gloom are seen a mass of running and tottering people, a lunging of driven beasts, all making for the keep within. The men-at-arms are rushing to the battlements and impatient wardens stand at the chains of the drawbridge. At last with loud creaking it is drawn up and none too soon, before the hills around seem suddenly to become alive with warriors and woe betide the unfortunate who has not crossed the bridge in time.

The word blackmail stems from the activities of gangs of thugs who plagued the inhabitants of the English-Scottish border zone in those days of long ago. They lived in caves and fastnesses of various sorts which could only be reached by gang-ways or secret paths in treacherous and swampy areas. They became known as Moss Troopers because of the brown color of their apparel which blended with that of the terrain in which they operated.

They levied harsh tribute on farmers in return for pledges that they would not be molested by Moss men. This tribute consisted of "black and white mail."* The "black mail" was represented by black cattle and the "white mail" by white cattle. A sword thrust or noose hanging from a convenient tree branch, a burned farm and stolen cattle constantly threatened those humbler folk who defied them. The fear of the Moss men sealed the lips of many persons who knew the secret ways leading through the bogs to the freebooters' lairs, thus hampering punitive operations by king's men.

In many instances the more stouthearted citizens took matters into their own hands and organized retaliatory posses, whenever possible using bloodhounds. It is recorded that in numerous cases the farmers and tradesmen obtained permission from the authorities to levy a special tax to purchase and maintain one or more bloodhounds for tracking down these gangsters in a kind of embryonic K-9 operation.

"While very often the hunted men were bloody from some type of fray, the presence of blood was not a necessity to the chase," Richardson points out. "The body scent of the fugitive was in itself sufficient. . . . The strange, throttled howling sob of

* Mail in England and Scotland in ancient times meant any payments secured by extortion, whether in money, animals or goods. Our modern word blackmail stems from one of the combinations of words used during this period. "White mail" probably was interchangeable with the other combination in the past but ultimately vanished from the English language.

the hounds when in full cry must often have been heard on those dreary northern heaths and with the unfettered hunting conditions of soil and air the result must have been, on many occasions, a practical certainty."

A Bishop Ross who lived in that era has left an interesting account of how the Moss Troopers operated and how they were hunted. He wrote:

They come out of their own borders in the night by troops over inaccessible places and infinite windings. In the daytime they refresh their horses in proper hiding-places and conceal themselves till they arrive by favour of darkness at the places of their destination. When they have got their booty they return home again by long circuits and pathless ways. The more capable any of them is to guide through these wastes, windings and precipices in midnight darkness, the greater honour is he held in for his skill; and so cunning are they that they seldom suffer their booty to be taken from them, unless they are sometimes seized by their enemies, who follow close at their heels and track them by scent of dogs.*

In one episode, recounted by another historian of the time, the hounds themselves went off on a surprise tangent with very successful results.

A party of armed cavaliers was chasing a hare with bloodhounds when the dogs suddenly began milling around, "betraying the greatest excitement." The cavaliers were puzzled since no quarry was visible and up to that point the hounds had been enthusiastically following what certainly was a hare's trail, the horsemen pounding after them. Suddenly one of the hounds lifted his muzzle, questingly sniffed the air and gave tongue repeatedly. Apparently he had smelled something which interested him far more than the hare's trail.

The hound bounded forward toward a narrow pathway in

---

* This account has been adapted from the Elizabethan English of the original.

nearby bushes. Followed by other hounds and riders, the dog led them through the narrow path in the shrubbery, down a hill, through a grove of trees, across a small stream, and stopped with a loud howl at the mouth of a cavern. It was dusk and the glow of a fire was reflected in the rocky entrance to the cave. The cavaliers dismounted and brandishing pistols and swords rushed into the cave, fairly certain that this was a Moss Trooper lair.

In the center of the cave an old hag was stirring a pot over a fire, a terrified child clinging to her skirts. Sitting on a rock nearby, a huge man in tattered clothing arose with a shout, brandishing the sword he had been polishing. The intrusion was so swift and apparently so unexpected, the odds so heavy, that he almost immediately dropped his weapon and sullenly surrendered. The hunters had captured the leader of one of the most troublesome bands in the area, whose men had succeeded in keeping their principal stronghold, this cave, a secret for a long time.

The captured leader was hanged after a summary trial and his execution brought an end to the activities of this group of outlaws.

In more modern times, roughly the 1700's and the early 1800's, a somewhat specialized type of bandit plagued European countries, labeled highwayman in England. He is a particularly storied figure in English song and story and paintings, a romantic daredevil in a long caped cloak, tricorne hat and booted trousers, mounted on a fine steed, armed with big horse pistols. The number of this type of outlaw increased as more and more stagecoaches came into use on regular runs between towns and cities. His modus operandi was not unlike that of our Wild West stagecoach and train robbers. Plundering stagecoaches was their preferred activity. Materializing suddenly on a highway, generally at night, face masked, pistols cocked, they were the dread of all coachmen and passengers. As a whole, they were not a very murderous breed and usually got their loot without any bloodshed.

Probably the most daring highwayman of all time was Dick Turpin, whose name is a household word in Britain, the subject of innumerable stories and poems, many of them wildly glamorized.

On one occasion debonair Dick, for once dismounted, was pursued deep into a wooded area in Yorkshire by bloodhounds and mounted king's men. A swift runner, he completely eluded his pursuers, although the hounds were hot on the trail. Just how he did it is not known. Possibly he climbed a tree and swung himself to the branches of other trees, dropping to the ground after he had covered a satisfactory distance aloft. Probably the hounds were not very well trained animals with no expert handlers present for proper recasting. The sands ran out for Dick in 1739 when he was thirty-three years old. He was captured and executed in that year at York.

A much more beautiful dog than the bloodhound also has its place in the annals of law enforcement with the aid of canines. This is the popular collie. Although not favored for police work today, in the past it proved a staunch if unofficial aide to policemen, notably in England and Scotland. One dog of this breed became involved in a battle royal on the outskirts of London in the early 1900's, a fight which might have proved fatal for a constable but for the presence of the dog. Richardson tells the story:

One constable I know personally started life in Ireland, tending his father's sheep. To work a dog was therefore quite instinctive with him. When he came over to this country [England] and joined our police, it was the most natural thing in the world that he should bring his female collie Maisie with him. With a little special training under her master she was soon able to understand that lurking individuals, not sheep, were her prime concern.

One night this policeman and his canine companion [there was no official dog division at the time] were patrolling the streets of London when the policeman became suspicious of a man walking ahead of them. The constable called on the man to stop. He paid no attention and made off on the run. The policeman unleashed Maisie, gave her a pursuit order, and she bounded off. She caught the man's flying coattails. His efforts to free himself just gave the constable sufficient time to come up with him. A terrible corps-à-corps ensued between the two. The policeman's assailant was very powerful and was armed with a club. The area was a rather lonely one, the buildings nearby unoccupied at that time.

He broke away once more and again constable and dog pursued. This time they overtook him near some houses in a residential zone. The fight between the two men started again but the fugitive soon began to get the upper hand. All the time, however, the dog was dancing around the attacker barking and snapping at him. People in houses nearby were aroused by the noise and help soon was forthcoming for the constable. The fugitive was subdued and arrested. Maisie's master was badly hurt and had to be hospitalized for a spell. There is little doubt that Maisie's barking alarm saved him from death.

Richardson penned some advice regarding the use of dogs in police work which generally holds good today in spite of new training techniques and high-speed transportation and communications facilities.

"The dogs which are to be used for police work, whether as trackers or patrol animals, must on no account be savage," he said.

He maintained that the "sense of responsibility towards the master" must be highly developed in a dog.

. . . . The sense of uniform will soon develop and it will comprehend that its duty is towards the service (police or army) and not to the individual. . . . I have found that in all these public services it is better to use the native breeds of our country rather than those of other lands as in every case dogs and men of the native race understand each other best. . . . In England the motto of the police dog is defence. Along this line the police dog has a wide channel to exercise its intelligence, its detective and guarding powers. If its master . . . is attacked the attitude of obligation towards the master will produce a spirit of ardent defence in the right type of dog and will ill-betide anyone who seeks to injure him. . . . It is not desirable that human beings should be liable to physical attack from a dog. . . . To create a desirable impression it is better that the animals should be of a good size. Apart from the effect of a powerful dog going on duty, the fact that its weight is available as a means of attack or defence is a useful factor in the situation.

Richardson did not favor use of the German shepherd dog for police work but his view would probably be different today when the record of the Alsatian is outstandingly satisfactory.

The police dog which is in use in the continent is of too savage a disposition for the needs of our police. Being a sheep dog* this animal trains well and can be made obedient to orders, but there always is this strain of ferocity which is very difficult to eradicate and which breaks out at times in a dangerous manner. As a matter of fact it has been found that such animals are far from satisfactory and frequently by their aggressive conduct arouse public opinion against this method.

He said that the best technique for a policeman to follow was to keep his dog on the leash either all the time while on patrol or at all events until he thoroughly understood the animal's temper and disposition.

As to how far it would be safe for him to release the dog depends on the man himself to a great extent and the amount of understanding he possesses as to its control, also as to the length of time which it has actually been training with the police.

---

* Richardson probably was referring to a variety of sheep dog then in use, not specifically the Alsatian.

For patrolling the outskirts of great cities police dogs are excellent. The fact that they are there exerts a deterrent effect on crime of the theft class, as the detective powers of the constable are greatly enlarged by his having a good hearing and scenting dog with him.

One of the most unusual assignments ever undertaken by a dog expert was fulfilled by Richardson in 1907, an *Arabian Nights* cachet in the whole affair.

No less a person than the Sultan of Turkey, the notorious Abdul Hamid, requested Richardson to bring several dogs to Constantinople, for a fat purse, all expenses paid. They were needed, the Sultan's message said, to help Turkish guards and their dogs prevent "unauthorized persons" from entering the grounds of fabulous Yildiz Kiosk palace in the city (now Istanbul), a favorite residence of the potentate.

Edwin selected three dogs, a beautiful sable collie named Laddie, another collie named Quick, and a black and tan bloodhound, named Warrior. The four arrived in Constantinople from England in the early summer of that year via Orient Express.

Edwin's imports performed splendidly in tracking and guard work, their training and aptitude obviously far superior to that of the motley batch of palace animals. The bejeweled, perfumed Sultan, surrounded by notables of the court, attended some of the trials. He expressed pleasure over the dogs' performances. So did the guards—most of them giant eunuchs. Hamid was very courteous to the British visitor. Richardson received a handsome purse and the Order of Medjidie before returning to England by Orient Express, minus dogs.

During the visit Richardson wryly speculated on the real reason for the canine addition to the palace "security." There were residents of the palace—permanent ones—who probably viewed with mixed feelings the improved dog surveillance. The Sultan,

Edwin believed, needed some top-notch dogs to curb the activities of enterprising and daring Romeos seeking closer ties with these veiled residents, some of them very attractive.

They were the ladies of the royal harem.

There were 700 of them present at the time!

Dog attacks "criminal" in padded suit during training

> Whenever man is unhappy, God sends him a dog.
> —ALPHONSE DE LAMARTINE, French author and poet

5

The K-9 Trailblazers

ON a sunny day in the year 1920 a small crowd of men, women and children, dispersing in the streets of New York City after witnessing a parade, checked their strolling along a side street following a statement made by a burly man in civilian clothes.

The man was standing in the middle of the street near a corner, holding a big dog on leash. Answering a query from one of the passersby, he had told him he was a detective and that the dog was attached to the police department. In a loud, half-jocular voice, he added for the benefit of all present:

"If you folks are interested, hang around a minute and I'll give a demonstration, show you how good these dogs are under fire."

This immediately prompted all the passersby to halt on the sidewalk to observe the man and dog more closely. The dog itself was enough to arouse considerable interest, a Belgian sheep dog, not often seen in this country. Most of the onlookers knew that New York City police had been using trained dogs for more than a decade, principally in Long Island, but none had ever seen such an animal in action. It was all a newfangled thing in this country at the time. This promised to be an interesting sideshow to the parade—something worth watching. Possible nervousness as to personal safety was stilled by the detective.

"There'll be some banging, folks, but keep calm, only blank bullets this time."

The spectators and the detective little dreamed that tragedy was swiftly impending—one that would deal a serious blow to this country's man-dog police operations.

The plainclothesman unleashed the dog and ordered it to crouch down in the street a few paces away. Then he drew his revolver and fired, directing the weapon's barrel at a point over the dog's head. Almost simultaneously two other revolver shots rang out and the detective reeled and fell to the pavement. The startled crowd next beheld a patrolman running down the street to the spot where the man had fallen, gripping a revolver in his hand. The dog was circling the prostrate detective barking defiantly but the patrolman, who obviously knew the animal, succeeded in calming him. Then he bent down to examine the prone form. The detective was dead.

Too late he realized that the slain man was no thug but a detective on the force whom he knew well. It was a sad case of mistaken identity. Rounding a nearby corner he had clearly seen the man open fire on the dog, which he immediately recognized as one belonging to the police department. His field of fire clear of other persons, he had drawn his revolver and loosed the fatal shots, believing the detective whose back was turned to him was a roughneck trying to kill a police dog.

This tragedy, coupled with methods of handling the dogs in suburban areas which aroused public ire, caused complete cessation that year of all K-9 operations of the New York police.

New York City was the first to organize K-9 man-dog teams for police work in the United States. Its action was inspired by the successful dog operations in Ghent, Belgium. That city had begun using official man-dog teams in 1899. It is generally credited with being the pioneer in this sphere.

After studying accounts of the Ghent operation and increased use of dogs in law enforcement in Germany and France resulting from the Ghent move, General Bringham, Police Commissioner of New York City, decided to try combating crime with trained canines.

In 1907 Bringham sent a representative named George Wakefield to Ghent to study the possibilities on the spot and return to the United States with dogs for breeding and operational purposes. Wakefield came back in 1908 with six Belgian sheep dogs, the type used in Ghent. This dog must not be confounded with the German shepherd then being bred, although like the Alsatian they are large and have a fairly thick coat.

Records are vague as to just what was done with these dogs, which included females, when they arrived in New York City. Apparently some of the animals were quite young and some time elapsed while they were being trained. The females, it is believed, were used for breeding purposes and the best puppies selected as additions to the unit. It is known that by 1911 New York City had 16 dogs in operation of this breed or crossbred animals.

The Ghent system was relatively sound. The dogs there patrolled on leash virtually all of the time. To avoid possible unpleasant incidents involving innocent persons, the dogs were equipped with special muzzles. This curb fitted somewhat loosely but sufficiently tight to make it difficult for a dog to shake itself free from it. By a means of a special string a handler, faced with a critical emergency, could immediately cause it to fall off the dog's head.

There were, however, serious flaws in the Ghent procedures. In line with Belgian thinking, the dogs were subjected to training intensifying their aggressiveness toward anyone not in a policeman's uniform or a plainclothesman known to them. The muzzle apparently was never used by the New York police. Even if it had been used, it never could have constituted complete protection for persons attacked by an angry dog of the larger type. The whole modern conception that a law enforcement dog must constantly be under complete control was a nebulous affair at that time. Trouble was bound to ensue.

It is doubtful that the dogs were each assigned their own special police "master" handler. Probably they went out on patrol with whatever policeman was available on a particular tour of duty, often a man who hardly knew the animal and had little liking for the species in general. The teams were used almost exclusively to patrol various Long Island residential areas, on duty from 11 P.M. to 7 A.M. During these tours of duty the dogs frequently were unleashed and permitted to roam loose in the zone, the handler casually following the dog, hoping that the animal somehow would corral a nocturnal evildoer. The results can easily be imagined. Some arrests of suspects did occur and the action proved justified, the dog largely instrumental in the capture. But the outcome was nightmarish for many law-abiding citizens strolling in the streets or entering their homes late at night. A large dog roaming loose at night is a potentially troublesome presence, except in the case of a particularly friendly or enfeebled animal. The police dogs charged many totally innocent persons, men and women. In some cases the officer was close enough to call off the dog and the victims merely suffered a bad fright. In other instances, though, injuries occurred from falls or bites. Complaints mounted through the years but the police felt the dogs were helpful and added some canines to the force, including Airedales and some native houndlike dogs. By 1920 the New York unit had some 22 dogs enrolled. But the training and modus operandi had not changed much. The fatal shooting of the detective plus the complaints of irate citizens constituted a deathblow to this pioneering K-9 unit in the United States, and somewhat reluctantly the police abandoned it in 1920.

In tracing the history of K-9 operations throughout the world, the action undertaken by the French port city of Saint-Malo centuries ago is believed to be the first instance in which dogs were officially used for law enforcement in regular patrols. Their activity was limited to a specific part of the town and the operation was not as important as that undertaken by Ghent in modern times.

Harried by robberies and violent brawls in dock areas where important naval installations were located, the city's authorities in the early 1300's formed a type of canine corps to maintain order in the zone. Various dogs known to be good guard animals and reasonably obedient were selected for the work and began patrolling the area, accompanied by armed citizens. The program proved successful and was continued until the year 1770 when an unfortunate accident occurred. In that year one

of the larger and more aggressive dogs, roaming the area unleashed in the dark, attacked and killed a young naval officer
walking through the zone after curfew. This caused abandonment of the program. Nonetheless the dogs of Saint-Malo have
become a legend in France and their memory is honored to this
day in the official insignia of the city.

During the 1400's the picturesque town and abbey of Mont-
Saint-Michel, France, famed as tourist attraction in modern
times, was presented with a selected group of guard dogs by
King Louis XI. These were stationed as sentries along the walls
and at the main gates.

The Ghent police dog program, although abandoned in recent years, constitutes an extremely important milestone in K-9
law enforcement. It came into being at the turn of the century
through the untiring efforts of the then Ghent Police Commissioner E. Van Wesemael, who loved dogs and was convinced
they could be useful in the work of his department. Van Wesemael, a handsome, intelligent man, his face adorned with the
Vandyke beard popular in that day, won the needed approval
from his superiors and in March of 1899 his department purchased three dogs with promising capabilities. During the summer and fall seven more dogs were added to the force. All were
subjected to about two months' training, embodying the best
principles evolved up to that time. Shortly before Christmas,
1899, when Ghent had a population of about 175,000 within
its 10 square miles, 37 police dogs, most of them Belgian sheep
dogs, were on patrol between 10 P.M. and 6 A.M. Usually a
policeman made his rounds with two dogs on leash and was able
to control the pair without undue trouble. All the patrolling
was beamed at areas where crime was most prevalent.

As far as the authorities were concerned the experiment
proved a success and it won general public approval in spite of
some unpleasant but not serious incidents involving innocent
persons.

Approximately one year after the program's inception, the Police Commissioner requested the city's burgomaster to permit his department to acquire six additional dogs, a request which was soon granted. The letter in which he made the request is an historic document in K-9 annals. After pointing out that the use of dogs saved the expense of hiring additional policemen, Wesemael made various statements which hold good today and in the future.

. . . I am not certain that a night policeman, who is operating in the suburbs, far from any help whatever, dare intervene when he sees a crime committed by several criminals. He cannot go as far and as fast as criminals, after being on duty for several hours. The criminal meditating a crime dresses lightly so that he can flee more swiftly if this be necessary. A dog works a long time on duty cheerfully and he is able to follow a fugitive much more rapidly than a man. The dog is endowed with acute qualities of scent and hearing and can easily get into any place and examine it without his presence being suspected and thus surprise the criminal. In carrying out such a search a policeman probably would be heard. If the criminal, thanks to his agility, succeeds in jumping over an obstacle or swimming away, a dog can stop him; the policeman would be hampered because of his heavy uniform and perhaps he could not swim.

What I am anxious to do is to fulfill as completely as possible this want, so as to prevent crimes. Of course I do not hope to prevent all crimes—that would be an impossibility: we can only unite all our efforts in hindering them. . . .

By 1906 about 120 men, working with some 60 dogs, were patrolling various areas of Ghent. The operation aroused interest abroad and one English expert noted in an article in 1907:

It has become apparent that night crimes, even in the worst quarters of Ghent, have almost disappeared. Cunning ruffians had often contrived to outwit the solitary patrol, but these big, swift, silent-footed and sagacious sheep dogs inspire terror in the most desperate evildoers.

Meanwhile, the study of dog training, breeding and dog-man team work in law enforcement was proceeding apace in Germany. Today that country's contribution to the perfection of K-9 techniques both in peace and war is considered by many experts to be the most important in history.

The Germans were the first to adopt programs based on the Ghent operation and by 1910 more than 600 towns in Germany were using officially enrolled police dogs.

German breeders were responsible for creation of the highly intelligent Doberman pinscher and German shepherd dogs, both outstanding aides in police and military operations. The German shepherd was developed in the late 1800's by the noted German breeder, Max von Stephanitz, who evolved this animal by crossbreeding German sheepherding and cattle-driving varieties.

In the very beginning the Germans realized that the German shepherd was the best animal for police work as far as they were concerned, the Doberman taking second place. They also took an important step at the turn of the century to ensure continued careful breeding and to popularize this dog. They created the Verein fuer Deutsche Schaeferhunde (The Society for German Shepherd Dogs) which is still in existence today. Its advice on purchase of these dogs and suggestions on training methods have proven of immense value to police departments envisaging K-9 operations throughout the years.

Another German move occurred after World War I in which thousands of German dogs were used in the battle zones, the biggest war dog utilization in that conflict. In 1920 a special school manned by experts was established at Gruenheide, Germany, devoted entirely to the training of canine policemen, its rules and requirements very exacting.

Here the dogs were instructed in basic obedience, tracking, searching, obtaining assistance, and controlled attack patterns in obedience to verbal commands and signals. From this school came the plans and criteria for other training centers in various countries. Much of the training system used today in canine corps has been adopted with little change from the Gruenheide concepts.

In the years immediately preceding World War I the use of dogs for police work spread to other cities in Belgium and took hold in France, Britain, Italy and the Austro-Hungarian Empire. It is difficult to pinpoint developments in these and other countries in this embryonic phase, which in a general sense extended from 1900 to 1945. In many cases detailed records were not kept or were lost in wartime years. Exchange of information on this subject between police departments in various countries was very slight. Some towns and cities, as in the case of New York City, found trained dogs to be useful aides and then for one reason or another dropped the entire project.

Two world wars within the first half of this century dislocated the pattern of canine police operations. Trained animals working with the police were swallowed up by war dog pools, notably in France, Germany, and Britain. Some fairly important developments occurred in the period between the two world conflicts in Europe and elsewhere but such programs really gained scope after the end of World War II, far exceeding the development achieved in the years prior to World War I and in the twenties and thirties.

The success of K-9 police operations in Europe after World War II kindled wide interest among police officers here, and one K-9 department after another was started. In each case principles followed by London's police constituted the guideline for these special divisions. In some cases American police officers as a preliminary move studied the Scotland Yard's methods in visits to London. The Yard from time to time has provided trained dogs to some of our K-9 divisions.

Baltimore, Maryland, police were the first to launch a major program, which today groups 52 highly trained male German shepherds. Recruiting of the dogs started in 1956, 15 dogs to start with, the operation directed by a former American military dog trainer. By 1957 the experiment was considered a success and the K-9 corps was formally incorporated in the police force. The Baltimore unit is still considered a showcase corps in this country and its organization is closely studied by American and foreign experts at frequent intervals.

The most important K-9 departments in action in this country in 1965 numbered 28, located as follows:

Alexandria and Richmond, Virginia; Baltimore, Maryland; Chicago, Illinois; Atlanta, Georgia; Birmingham, Alabama; Boston, Massachusetts; Cleveland, Ohio; Dallas, Texas; Deleware State Police; Denver, Colorado; Houston, Texas; Jackson, Mississippi; Kansas City, St. Louis, and Springfield, Missouri; Kingman, Arizona; Las Vegas, Nevada; Miami, Florida; New Orleans, Louisiana; Philadelphia, Pennsylvania; San Francisco and Pomona, California; Reno, Nevada; St. Paul, Minnesota; Salt Lake City, Utah; Washington, D.C.; Witchita, Kansas, and Hartford, Connecticut.

New York City and Los Angeles, California, are notable exceptions in this roster of the more important divisions. It is possible that these two major cities will adopt K-9 programs in the future but at the time of this writing there are no indications that such moves are impending. There are no available overall statistics on the number of smaller units in the country such as those in Nassau and Suffolk counties in Long Island.

In a number of cases, aside from the early New York experiment, K-9 operations were tried in this country and then abandoned for various reasons. Eight German shepherds were used by police in Detroit, Michigan, in 1917 but in 1919 the program was terminated. The dogs, it was claimed, failed to help make any arrests and had been found of no assistance in tracking criminals. Nine years later Detroit reactivated the program with 12 dogs patrolling residential areas but in 1941 it again was scrapped.

Berkeley, California, had a number of Doberman pinschers working with policemen in the thirties but the project came to an end shortly before World War II. Police officials cited the special expenditures involved and vicious streaks in some of the dogs as being some of the reasons for the cessation of the program.

In July, 1954, the police of Dearborn, Michigan, put four teams into action but disbanded them after four months of operation without any unfavorable incident. The police said the city did not lend itself to the use of police dogs since it consisted of 96 percent homeowners, with very few drifters and virtually no juvenile or gang problems.

The dogs were sold to Portland, Oregon, police in May, 1955, after that department had decided to try the system. Portland activated a total of 15 teams grouping nine German shepherds and six Dobermans. One year after its inception, this operation also went by the board. Several reasons were given: the dogs were trained to work with one particular officer and it was time-consuming and expensive to retrain a dog to work with a new handler; the training of both men and dogs was never-ending and the use of the animals caused multiple administrative problems, it was said.

Bloodhounds have been used for many years in this country in units officially attached to state police. It is debatable whether these operations can be classified as complete K-9 undertakings. These dogs are used only for tracking, seeking escaped prisoners and missing persons, almost invariably outside town or city limits, at their best in open country. They are not trained for the varied duties of a real police K-9 dog. However, they have done excellent work in their particular line as such dogs did in England at one time.

Since 1938 the New York State Police have kept bloodhounds to assist in searches for criminals, missing persons, notably youngsters, lost hunters and others. Vermont State Police and Maine State Police have also found these fine trackers useful since 1953 and 1960 respectively. They are working for the police in a number of other states in coping with similar problems.

At the time of this writing the New York State Police have nine bloodhounds attached in varying numbers to troops at Hawthorne, Oneida, Malone and Batavia. One of the outstanding dogs goes by the name of Mack the Knife, after the famous character in *The Threepenny Opera*. There is nothing sinister about Mack, however. In nine years of service to the state, Mack has participated in about 500 searches for missing persons, virtually all of them very successful. In spite of his breed's lugubrious expression, he is a good-natured, affectionate animal and has never physically injured anyone. He is a particular favorite of children who got lost and whom he helped find. Since these dogs are not trained in aggressiveness, young visitors are freely allowed to pet him, all of which he accepts with dignity and good humor.

"These dogs are always kept on a leash when we are on tracking missions, even though we know they are not vicious in any way," Trooper Donahue, Mack's handler said in a recent interview. "The best experiences in my book occur when you go out and a child is lost. It gives special pleasure to a handler to be able to find the child with his dog."

Virtually all dogs are liable to show resentment if master or mistress shows favoritism for another dog and they are in a position to realize it. Bloodhounds are particularly sensitive in this matter, especially when tracking is under way. A bloodhound seeing another dog put on the trail while he is held back is apt to give loud voice to his displeasure. Aware of this fact, Sergeant William Horton of the New York State Police on one occasion executed a neat psychological ruse to help New Jersey police round up a dangerous criminal.

The criminal, who came from the South, had killed a New Jersey state trooper and then fled into a heavily forested, sparsely populated area in that state. The man, who had a long record, was well-armed. New Jersey police called Troop K at Hawthorne and Horton hurried off to join the other state's troopers in their search.

Police were strung all around the forested area. When William and his two dogs joined one of the units at the edge of the forest, he had a plan. The man came from the South, that was important. Something new might be tried.

Going into action immediately, he tied one of his dogs securely to the tailboard of his sedan. Then he took off with the other bloodhound straining at the leash and disappeared in underbrush and thickets.

The remaining hound made a desperate effort to break its bonds and then sat on its haunches looking reproachfully at the men around it. Then it burst into a spine-chilling lament of frustration, jealousy, and deep-seated resentment. It was a baying that could be heard over a wide area.

Deep in the wilderness, the killer heard the lament and shuddered. What! Bloodhounds after him. Resting at the moment in a thicket, he rose hurriedly and started a desperate flight through the forest. Working his way through the thickets and trees from cover to cover, he finally made a last dash across a clearing and a woods road—right into the gun sights of buddies of the slain trooper.

Word that he had been captured was conveyed almost immediately to the sector where the dogs were on duty. Almost simultaneously and to the astonishment of the onlookers, Bill and his hound nonchalantly stepped out of the nearby thickets.

That was as far as they had been, a few feet out of sight of the tied-up animal! Horton's hunch had been a good one. The anguished baying, its connotations particularly terrifying to a Southern felon, had been enough to provoke utter panic in the fugitive.

Although New York City has no K-9 division, dogs are playing an increasing role as effective guards throughout the metropolis. Besides department store patrols in such a store as Macy's, they are helping apartment house guards protect big housing developments against prowlers. Trained dogs have been recruited for work in the Bronx Zoo, a somewhat unusual assignment. They are there to protect the zoo animals against sundry types of molestation or teasing by humans visiting the establishment. Guards at the Brooklyn Botanical Gardens, plagued by vandals, began patrolling the gardens with a trained German shepherd in the fall of 1965 and expect to acquire others in the future. With the dog on the scene vandalism has been practically nil.

To what extent trained dogs are being used in police work in the divided land which was Germany could not be satisfactorily ascertained by this author. I did not try to contact officials in Communist East Germany but did seek data by correspondence from Inter Nationes, a German organization supplying information of all types involving West Germany. In replying Inter Nationes forwarded a letter from the Verein fuer Deutsche Schaeferhunde with headquarters at Augsburg.

This letter contained some interesting information but no estimates on the number of police dogs in action were forthcoming nor were any accounts of their exploits in recent years available. Somewhat surprisingly, the message disclosed that West German authorities maintain secrecy regarding the achievements of dogs in police work. The Verein's letter, dated February 17, 1966, reads as follows:

The State Police Dog Training School at Gruenheide was dissolved shortly before the end of World War II. The school was not reactivated after the end of the war since the police dog organization [Ed.: meaning the use of dogs in police work] was decentralized after World War II. This resulted in part from the division of Germany into east and west zones. In the republic's government [West Germany] there are only three governmental departments using dogs, the customs, government railways and for the past five years the Bundeswehr [Army]. Establishment and operation of police dog units is in the hands of local authorities in the various areas.

Answering some of your questions we can give the following information.

Successful achievements of police dogs in police work are seldom made public in the German Bund Republic [West Germany]. The various official bodies using such dogs have decided upon this policy for definitive reasons. They have also warned against newspaper accounts of such achievements. They know that newspapers must have their quota of articles and often are not prone in many cases to stick to the truth.

In the republic the German shepherd in 98% of the cases is the canine favored as a working animal. There is no doubt that various official bodies often have had outstanding successes with dogs. However, we cannot supply detailed and entirely trustworthy reports on such accomplishments.

The Verein continues to be a very active organization in all questions pertaining to the development and training of the German shepherd dog and is frequently consulted by police authorities throughout the world.

In our big neighbor country, Canada, the famous Royal Canadian Mounted Police has been using dogs effectively in law enforcement since the K-9 program was initiated in the 1930's. The dogs and their handlers are stationed at key points from coast to coast throughout Canada. Here, too, the German shepherd has won perference but other types of dogs have also performed well on various occasions.

These teams are in readiness at all times, night or day, to

respond to requests for assistance in locating missing persons, lost or stolen articles, illicit liquor supplies, evidence at scenes of crimes, trailing criminals and guarding prisoners or evidence.

The Royal Bank of Canada in 1955 awarded a special collar with a laudatory inscription to Silver, a handsome female German shepherd of the Mounties. The collar was presented in gratitude for the important role played by the dog in a major bank holdup at Burnaby, near Vancouver, B.C., on January 13, 1955.

On that day three hooded desperadoes held up the Burnaby branch of the Royal Bank of Canada and made off with about $27,000. A massive police hunt started immediately and the robbers, abandoning their car, fled into the countryside near the town, which has a population of 80,000. Police reinforcements were called in, including Silver and her handler, stationed at Cloverdale, 20 miles distant. The gunmen were run to ground by the police in a wide dragnet that day. During the hunt Silver's fine nose, following the scent of the bandits, was immensely useful to the police in finding the bulk of the money. This had been abandoned at various points by the fugitives, most of the loot in plastic bags. One of the desperadoes had discarded an overcoat in a field and from this Silver obtained a good scent in the very beginning. Speedily the dog located one plastic bag containing $15,000 and another holding some $2,000, all in cash. The whole operation was a spectacular piece of police work, materially aided by the alertness and cooperation of local residents. All of the loot except some $98 had been recovered by nightfall, the canine also helpful in locating the other bundles of money.

Another RCMP Alsatian performed very well—under the surface of the earth. In the late afternoon of January 16, 1956, the dog and his handler were hurriedly summoned to aid in a search for three youths reportedly lost in an abandoned coal mine near Sydney Forks, Nova Scotia, where the RCMP has a dog breeding center. The trio had been seen entering the mine in the morning of that day and had subsequently not been sighted or heard from. Search parties had failed to locate them.

The dog was lowered about 40 feet to the main tunnel and started searching with his handler and some other men. There were no lighting facilities in the mine and portable lamps had to be used. Bad air soon caused the lamps to go out. A network of tunnels added further difficulties to the search. The Alsatian followed the main shaft for a quarter of a mile when he suddenly became interested in one of the side tunnels. Upon entering this tunnel the searchers found the youths, whose ages ranged from eight to ten, huddled together, exhausted and very scared. They had become completely lost in the dark mine and might well have perished in it but for the dog.

One of the smallest countries in the world is operating one of the largest K-9 divisions in existence, if area and population are taken into consideration. This is Denmark, population 5,000,-000, its area some 17,000 square miles (Greenland and the Faroe Islands not included). This kingdom was one of the pioneers in the enrollment of dogs for police work. The dog operations began in 1907 in the wake of the Ghent trailblazing and have been expanded ever since. As of 1965, Denmark had a highly trained K-9 force in the police of 150 dogs. Ten of these are Rottweilers and Doberman pinschers, the rest Alsatians.

About 50 of the dogs are on duty in the capital, Copenhagen, and its vicinity, the remainer elsewhere in the country. The training methods and general procedure are similar to the British system and ours. In refresher exercises at regular periods handlers and dogs are often confronted with problems they have never tackled before but which might occur in police work. These are usually particularly complex but in most cases a dog and its master succeed in solving them from scratch because of meticulous training. Denmark has a unique magazine, published monthly, entitled *The Police Dog*, providing interested readers with varied information on canine law enforcement. It has been published for the past 50 years. In 1966 its monthly circulation was 2,200 copies.

The statistics for Denmark in 1965 were impressive. The dogs were in action in at least 2,433 cases. During these operations 596 persons were arrested as a direct result of canine assistance. According to information received from the Copenhagen police department during this period, the dogs were used 76 times in coping with street riots—indicating that the Danish police find them helpful in such control. The riots were not extremely serious, however. The animals also materially helped the police in coping with tavern brawls, some of which were of a violent nature.

One incident shows that a trained police dog can be effective in a special sphere—handling the noncriminal insane. This episode occurred in the Copenhagen zone. Two ambulance men from a mental hospital were ordered to pick up a deranged man at his home and bring him to the hospital. When one of the ambulance men entered the hall of the house the man, suddenly gone berserk, attacked him with a carving knife. Slightly cut, the ambulance man fled to the outside and called for police. The madman meanwhile had locked himself in and could be heard shouting demoniacally inside his dwelling.

A police handler and dog arrived on the scene in a radio car and the front door was broken open. The handler and the animal, held on leash, entered the building and located the man in a room. Still holding the knife, he shouted threats at the intruders. Ordered to attack, the dog seized the knife arm and the madman was quickly subdued. He suffered only minor injuries.

In another episode two handlers and two dogs sped to the grounds of a big factory where a burglar alarm had gone off in the night. Here the handlers were confronted with a puzzler which they solved with a neat ruse. The intruder, or intruders, had many avenues of escape, the buildings and grounds covering a large area. It would be difficult to make a capture unless the hunted became convinced that the zone was being surrounded by many searchers. The two handlers first made their dogs bark loudly at one point, then ran with their canines to another, and still another, the barking repeated. The dogs then were unleashed and told to search. They soon accomplished their mission. They nailed three men hiding under a tarpaulin in a particularly dark corner. The trio was promptly placed under arrest for intended burglary. Convinced that police and dogs were closing in from all sides, they had abandoned all plans of escaping from the area and had hoped that by hiding they could escape later.

These and many other episodes lend weight to a saying widely quoted in K-9 operations, especially by lawbreakers who have rued the day dogs were put on their track:

"You can argue with a policeman but not with a dog."

"Il Gigante" of Italy—who gets top billing in the next chapter —certainly was a dog no one would wish to argue with.

Maimone and Dox

The misery of keeping a dog, is his dying so soon;
but to be sure, if he lived for fifty years, and then
died, what would become of me?

—Sir Walter Scott

6

"Il Gigante"

WHENEVER Salvatore Suriano of Rome, Italy, gazed into the window of a small but elegant shop in the Via Cola di Rienzo his determination to become one of the haves instead of the have-nots hardened. Here, beyond the glass, was

114

the passport, or passports, that finally would usher him through the gates of *dolce vita* land, his pockets bulging with lire.

During the spring of 1958 Salvatore would frequently stop his random strolling, a favorite activity of his, and beam his shifty eyes on the store's shining window and the tastefully displayed wares beyond it. The glitter in his eyes matched that of the displays and the neatly printed price tags made his mouth water. Thus far there had been no *dolce vita* based on financial affluence in the bumpy career of Salvatore. Ways and means of earning an honest lira from a tender age had been distasteful to this Roman, now in his late twenties. Thievery was an easier way out and that had become his specialty over the years. He was one of Rome's petty burglars. By the spring of that year he had scored a few minor successes but the pickings had been slim. In some instances these operations had brought him into un-amiable contact with the Rome police and cooling-off periods in various jails.

The police had generally been indifferent toward him during 1958 but his financial outlook was particularly bleak this spring. The funds from various small hauls which he had discreetly consummated during the past winter without police interference were near zero.

Enough of this small-time stuff, Salvatore reflected with increasing moodiness. The cure for his bitterness was in this jewelry store in the Via Cola di Rienzo. Just a good bagful would be sufficient. The tactical situation from his viewpoint was not bad. Next to the store was a motion picture theater, the Principe. He surmised that only a wall, apparently not too thick, separated the store from the theater. Formulating a plan of action, his preliminary "intelligence" work disclosed that the wall was indeed relatively thin. He also ascertained elatedly that an underground storeroom of the shop was adjacent to a basement of the theater that contained a furnace.

In March he decided that the planning stage was over. Carrying a small satchel containing diverse tools under his raincoat, Salvatore bought a ticket and entered the theater during a late show. He attracted no particular notice and succeeded in reaching the basement without arousing suspicion. Once there he opened his satchel and with the aid of a flashlight began chipping away at the wall between the theater and the shop.

The case of the missing button, one of the most extraordinary in K-9 annals, was now heading for a climax. The champion police dog of the world, "Il Gigante" (The Giant), better known as Dox, his name already legendary in Italy and elsewhere, was waiting in the wings for another call to action. So was his veteran handler, Brigadiere (Sergeant) Giovanni Maimone, the "Hercules Cop," both members of the Squadra Mobile (Flying Squad) of the Rome police.

An exceptionally large German shepherd weighing 140 pounds, Dox was a very senior citizen at that time, eighty-four years old if you figure seven human years to a dog's year of life. Twelve years of strenuous and dangerous living had not, however, lessened this dog's amazing capabilities, as he would soon prove.

Everything was proceeding smoothly in the basement when a night watchman in the theater heard faint tappings and headed downstairs.

Aware that someone was nearing the room, Salvatore doused his flashlight and hid behind the furnace. When the guard entered the room, the rogue jumped him, knocking his flashlight out of his hand. Both men grappled in the darkness. The watchman gave a shout but the picture was still on in a noisy talking sequence and nobody heard it. A quick knee thrust in the groin and a punch to the face from Salvatore brought the watchman writhing to the ground. Fearful that the man's shout had been heard, Salvatore swiftly gathered up his tools and fled the building through a side door and headed for another part of Rome. It is believed that, once in the street, he hurriedly left the tool case with an accomplice acting as a lookout and told him to decamp in another direction.

Although dazed and in some pain, the watchman soon managed to rise and get to a telephone upstairs. There he blurted out his story to police headquarters.

A police car of the Squadra Mobile screeched to a halt outside the Principe shortly after the phone alarm had gone through. Out of it tumbled Dox, his handler, holding him on a leash, and another policeman. About forty minutes had elapsed since the attack and the watchman, now in reasonably good shape, led the men and the dog downstairs. A quick glance at the hole in the wall convinced the police that it was not large enough for passage of a man's body although the thief had succeeded in piercing the partition. A rapid search of the basement room provided no interesting clues. There was one, however, a small one which had fallen into a crevice at the spot where the men had grappled. Perhaps Dox, who was busily sniffing around, perceived it and took note of it in his cunning brain. As far as Maimone was concerned, the paramount issue was for the dog to get a good human scent and follow it as quickly as possible. Realizing that the bandit had been in close physical contact with the watchman, Maimone prompted Dox to sniff the guard's clothing, hands and face. A few sniffs seemed to satisfy the canine sleuth and a determined tug in the direction of the room's door left no doubt in Maimone's mind that the dog had a good scent. There existed almost telepathic understanding in such matters between the two. Maimone gave him his head and without faltering Dox led the three men up the stairs and out into the street through the door used by the burglar.

Once outside, the dog determinedly led his master through street after street, the other two men bringing up the rear in the car. At one or two points the dog, nose to the ground, seemed to hesitate but only briefly. After a circuitous hunt of almost an hour Dox stopped before the door of a cellar in a dilapidated building in a tenement district of Rome at a considerable distance from the Principe theater. The policemen banged on the door and it was opened by a man in rumpled trousers and shirt. With a somewhat fearful glance at Il Gigante, he grumpily asked the policemen what was afoot. Without replying, the two policemen and the guard entered, Dox, still on leash, growling menacingly.

A brief interrogation and some sharp glances at the man's face almost immediately enabled the police to identify him as Suriano. The guard could only state that his height seemed to be the same as that of the man who had struck him down in the dark. Salvatore, gesticulating wildly, on the verge of tears, swore by bell, book and candle that he had been sleeping peacefully for many hours on the cot in a corner of the cellar room.

Suriano seemed so sincere in his protestations that in this case Maimone and his police companions concurred that Dox apparently was on the wrong track, that his aging senses had led him astray.

"Per Bacco, I should have known better," Maimone recalled in a special interview with a friend of this author in Rome in recent months. "Even I, with all my deep faith in my dog's judgment, was convinced that the man was being truthful. I chided Dox on the error, shaking my finger at him and warning him to be more careful next time. This did not impress my friend the corporal, for Dox had that rank in our force, as you may know. Instead of becoming docilely indifferent he growled at the man and then barked several times at me. As far as I was concerned this was a clear warning that he was not at all satisfied with developments. Then he looked at me seeming to say come on, now, follow me, you know me. I could not ignore this appeal. So back to the theater basement we went, the two of us in the car, leaving the other three in the cellar."

Once in the theater basement, Dox sniffed around again and picked up something which had fallen into a crevice near the furnace. It was a button and the dog laid it at Maimone's feet. This definitely was interesting, and man and dog hurried back to the tenement cellar. Entering the room, Dox sniffed at a closet door and barked excitedly. Maimone opened it and Dox without hesitating fastened his teeth on a raincoat and dragged it to the ground.

One of the raincoat's buttons was missing!

The button found by Dox corresponded to the others on the coat. Bits of material clinging to the newly discovered clue matched that of the coat.

This was damning evidence and Salvatore's protestations of innocence soon turned into a confession of guilt. The button had been torn off by the watchman in the scuffle but neither man had been aware that this had happened.

Salvatore cooled his heels in prison for almost three years thereafter. The police were convinced that an accomplice was involved but Salvatore, to his credit, did not blab and the supposed accomplice was not captured. The episode created quite a stir in the press and a new entry honoring the corporal was made on Rome police blotters. Maimone rewarded Dox with an ample dish of spaghetti and pork chops on the very day of the arrest, the favorite dish of Il Gigante.

Although this case was arresting from the detection angle, it was one of the least important as regards the type of crime involved. In his career which spanned more than a decade—the four-footed Sherlock played stellar roles in far more important cases. Some of them involved serious danger for handler and dog. Virtually every type of crime figured in his record: muggings, extortion threats, major burglaries, dope peddling, and murder. He and Maimone also tangled with Sicilian bandits of the infamous Salvatore Giuliano, an operation in which Maimone was seriously wounded.

When Dox was dismissed from the police force in 1961—a glaring case of official ingratitude and chicanery—he bore under his tawny hide the scars of seven bullet wounds. Part of his left ear was shot away in one bloody episode. In his spare time he bested all comers in annual international police dog meets in which top police canines from various countries participated.

It was Il Gigante who solved a murder case with international repercussions, the victim an American.

On the morning of October 31, 1960, a man was found dead in the front seat of a Volkswagen parked along the pebbly shoulder of the Via Tiburtina, ten miles outside Rome. Although there were no papers on the man, the police traced his identification through a set of international gasoline coupons in the glove compartment that were made out to his license-plate number.

Investigation disclosed that the man was one Norman Donges, a U. S. citizen. He was a retired colonel and apparently had worked for U. S. Army intelligence services during World War II. During the war he had made dozens of parachute missions into France as a spy and agent to aid the anti-Nazi underground. Part of his work had been done with the British Secret Service, under Walter K. Gottlieb, the legendary K-13. Gottlieb was found murdered in the bathtub of his Rome apartment on the Via Nomentana after the war in a case which never was satisfactorily cleared up.

When the body of Donges was found in the Volkswagen on the Via Tiburtina, police believed at first glance that the occupant had died of a heart attack. When the medical report on Donges showed that he had been strangled the news created a stir not only in Rome but in Paris, London and Washington as well.

Obviously this was no run-of-the-mill killing. From the White House, President Eisenhower ordered the FBI to get busy on the case. Sleuths from Paris and Scotland Yard and men of Interpol, the international police body, also got on the track.

Rome police let out all the stops. Altogether some 1,200 police-men and detectives were put on the case. Newspapers had a field day. Communist papers said it was a "politico-espionage mat-ter," while questions of atomic security were mentioned by the more conservative papers. European scandal sheets said the whole affair was linked with the international drug traffic.

At this time as in the past, the Rome police this year had a number of other trained dogs in its K-9 division but Dox and Maimone, the most famous team, were always given the top K-9 role in any important cases.

When it was announced that they were on the Donges case everyone in Rome speculated whether the *beniamino* (darling) of Italy—Dox—and his master or the other human investigators would solve the case. Virtually all were certain that Dox would do something vital.

He did not disappoint anyone.

Although it had appeared that Donges had died from natural causes when the body was first discovered in the early morning hours of October 31, the policemen first on the scene did not discard the possibility of foul play. As was customary, Maimone and Dox were on the scene almost immediately, by this time virtually standard procedure in cases where it might be impor-tant for the dog to pick up a scent.

For more than an hour the dog sniffed and smelled every inch of the Volkswagen and the clothes, hands, face and shoes of the dead man. Maimone stood quietly nearby. It was not necessary for him to give his dog any orders in such matters. Dox did not head off in any particular direction and ended his sniffing at a point near the car. Then he returned to his master's side. This indicated to Maimone that whatever scent his dog had picked up could no longer be followed, a person or persons possibly involved having departed in a car or on a motorcycle or bike. Deciding that his canine sleuth had completed his scenting operation, Maimone returned to Rome by car with Dox to await developments. The medical report was soon forthcoming and Maimone learned that a murder was involved.

From past experiences Maimone knew that in this case he could bank on an uncanny ability of Dox; to memorize a scent or various odors and use this knowledge days, weeks, even months, later. He was convinced the dog had picked up an important scent that day and knew what to do. Both man and dog immediately started patrolling the streets of Rome, Maimone giving Dox more or less a free hand in governing the direction to be followed. By covering many areas Dox thus would be given a chance to pick up the scent again—if it was in the capital.

The hunt lasted three days. During this time other policemen were arduously probing "espionage" and "atomic" angles. But not Dox. He had other ideas about solving the case. The dog kept leading Maimone first to one area of Rome and then another, mostly zones which had a fairly high incidence of crime. Maimone was convinced that his furry cop was following some type of lead prompted by mysterious instincts beyond human understanding. Yet October 31, November 1, November 2, passed with no results in spite of far-flung patrolling in the city. But Dox plodded on, sniffing, sniffing, searching, seemingly tireless, taxing the endurance of his master.

On the evening of November 3 Dox closed in for the kill, in the Piazza di Siena so familiar to American tourists. Numerous persons were either strolling or lounging in the square when Dox and Maimone on foot patrol entered it for a routine checkup as they had done in previous days. This square is by no means a criminal hangout, but all types of persons pass through or loiter in the square during a day's span and not all of them are respectable. Rounding a corner and entering the square, Dox suddenly tugged hard at his leash and pulled his master toward three young men, idly chatting at the corner of a building. A quick glance sufficed to tell Maimone that the trio belonged to the city's shadier strata. Shifty-eyed, pasty-faced, with hair and raffish clothing smelling of pomade and toilet water, they obviously were what Italians call *malviventi*—persons who live evilly.

When Maimone and his dog halted a few feet away from the trio, Dox began to bark furiously, his snout and eyes directed at one of the three youths. Quieting Dox with a brief command, Maimone jotted down their names. Not satisfied with their evasive answers to some of his questions and sure that his dog knew or sensed something, Maimone curtly ordered them to proceed with him to headquarters for further interrogation. Two of the youths were dismissed after interrogation but the one singled out by Dox was held and subjected to protracted grilling. This youth, seventeen-year-old Orante Cardarelli, had an unsavory record of idleness, nonpayment of debts, and disorderly behavior while drunk.

Finally, Cardarelli broke down and admitted that he had strangled Donges in a violent argument which occurred while both were under the influence of liquor. The quarrel assertedly resulted from Donges' refusal to remit money which Cardarelli claimed was owed him. Homosexuality was alleged to be involved.

This closed the case as far as the police were concerned. Orante was convicted and sent to prison. Pictures of Dox, grinning amiably, his damaged ear clearly visible, again dotted newspaper pages throughout the land. A few days later the corporal received his 11th gold medal for this feat at the behest of the city government. An engraving of the dog's head was on one side and the other bore the inscription: *Dox, world champion of police dogs.*

The new accomplishment of their *beniamino* did not provoke undue amazement in Italy. The Italians were still chuckling over an incident which occurred the previous year and put one more *malvivente* where he belonged—in prison.

Maimone always was a stickler in observing the birthdays of his beloved dog, which fell on May 4. A special treat—dining out—was invariably accorded the dog on this occasion. Main dish: spaghetti and pork chops. On Dox's birthday in 1959 Maimone, in spotless uniform, and his well-groomed dog began their birthday stroll. Occasionally the pair would halt and Maimone would smilingly answer the questions of interested passersby. Sometimes he permitted them to pet the dog, who basically had a friendly disposition, especially toward children.

On these occasions Maimone let Dox more or less choose whatever restaurant he liked. Dox was gastronomically fussy in this matter. The first three or four eateries they passed did not seem to interest the dog and Maimone reflected that perhaps at this moment he was not hungry. Rounding a corner, however, Dox suddenly showed great excitement and tugging at his leash headed for the door of a little trattoria in the middle of the block. Arriving at the door of the restaurant, Dox nudged it open and the pair entered the dining room.

Once inside the corporal went into action but victuals were not on his mind. Rushing past various startled diners on taut leash, he began circling one table, barking loudly. A husky, beetle-browed man, napkin stuffed into his shirt collar, was sitting at the table, halfway through a steaming dish of spaghetti and sausages.

In a few seconds Maimone realized that Dox had scored again. The man was a burglar captured by the brigadiere and Dox six years before in Turin. His whereabouts had been unknown after he had escaped from prison in Turin. Just where the dog had picked up the scent of the man on this, his thirteenth birthday, was a mystery to Maimone.

The brigadiere arrested the man and good-naturedly permitted him to finish his dish. Dox simultaneously got his reward in the kitchen—a huge dish of spaghetti and pork chops.

One of the world's outstanding authorities on animal psychology and behaviorism, the Italian writer Guglielmo Bonuzzi devotes a lengthy chapter to this dog and his master in his book *Gli Animali Si Vogliono Bene* (Animals Wish Each Other Well). Nowhere in the chapter does he express doubt regarding the phenomenal achievements of Il Gigante, which resulted from extraordinary animal intelligence and superb training. Bonuzzi writes:

Dox, the most famous and most decorated police dog in the world, was born on May 4, 1946, at Lichtenfels, in Germany. His was the 62nd generation of a genealogical tree which went back to the 19th century, its original sire a remarkable German shepherd dog named Nestor.

The name Dox was given to the dog by his master, Maimone. In view of his distinguished ancestry, Dox was fully entitled to an aristocratic appendage "von Coburger land"—a noble of that land, so to speak. . . . Everything about this dog, as a pup—piercing, intelligent eyes, sound reflexes, fine dark pelt with gold reflections—foreshadowed an uncommon tomorrow. But no one could foresee how amazing it would be with the aid of his trainer and owner, Maimone.

A friend of mine, Mrs. Kathleen Zammarano, an American woman married to an Italian, both residing in Rome, interviewed Maimone on several occasions during the writing of this book to obtain special information for this chapter.

Like Dox, Maimone was a May child, born on the 20th of that month in 1918 near Messina, Sicily, of peasant stock.

"I grew up physically strong and healthy," he told Mrs. Zammarano. "I always was crazy about dogs. At the age of four I brought home a little mongrel. He was a really lovable stray but he was not mine for long. The day following this adoption I found his body in front of our door. He had been stoned to death by some vicious youngsters. I would have gone after his killer knife or club in hand if I could have known who it was. I never did find out who did it.

"Weeping, I swore that I would own another pup. Over a period of years I had ten dogs, I loved them all. Some of them died from disease, others from age, some in accidents. I especially remember a black and white mongrel I named Bello. He was affectionate and intelligent. We understood each other marvelously. He had always accompanied me to school and waited patiently outside throughout school hours for me. We lived contentedly this way for two years. Then tragedy struck. My mother died and my father remarried. My stepmother became stepmother to the dog, too. At a time when I was not present she had Bello killed with two gunshots by a neighbor. I felt as if these shots had pierced my own heart. Besides loving dogs for themselves I owed the whole species deep gratitude. A dog had saved me from drowning when I was seven years old."

In his twenties, Giovanni decided he would become a policeman and was duly enrolled. The story of Maimone and Dox started in 1946 when Maimone was a policeman in Turin.

"Maimone did not have a dog at that time but he hankered after one and finally decided to do something about it," my Rome correspondent reported. "He was particularly interested in the German shepherd breed. He knew an Italian businessman who made regular trips to Germany. One day he asked him if he would bring him back from Germany a purebred pup of this breed purchased from a reputable kennel. Maimone's friend agreed and duly returned with a healthy pup. Maimone first beheld the dog—some forty days old—in June, 1946. As far as Maimone was concerned it was love at first sight and he formally became the frisky dog's master. He promptly named him Dox.

"Not everything was smooth sailing, however. There was a financial problem. Maimone had little ready cash. The price of the dog and transportation by rail amounted to 50,000 lire [about $80]. With the consent of his friend, Maimone decided to pay with promissory notes for small amounts covering a two-year period. There also was a housing problem. Maimone was living in the police barracks and had to keep Dox hidden. There were no provisos for dog pets around the barracks. Somehow Giovanni managed to keep Dox's presence secret. Dox was very cooperative in this, Maimone tells me. Always quite obedient and not prone to howl and bark when left alone.

"When Dox was some four months old—in the fall of 1946—a singular and rather diverting phase developed in the man-dog partnership. Already aware that his dog was endowed with exceptional intelligence and nasal perception, Maimone decided that the time was ripe for some special spare-time activity designed to expand his pocketbook. He bought a big suitcase, put his pet in it, and, after duty hours, made the rounds of the bars. This often lasted until two or three o'clock in the morning but the purpose was not alcoholic intake. The aim of the nocturnal jaunts was to pick up some cash to pay off his promissory notes. This, Maimone had decided craftily, might be achieved by having bar customers place bets with him on Dox's ability to follow a scent. Maimone knew that Dox's nose even at this tender age infallibly would lead him to a secreted object if he was given the opportunity to smell it and the person who hid it. The results were spectacular. Barflies gladly placed bets and thought they could outsmart the dog. Maimone never lost. Man and dog indulged in this 'sure bet' financial activity for several years. The promissory notes were all paid within a few months after Dox's arrival in Turin. Maimone estimates that Dox brought in some 7,000,000 lire [about $11,000] during this betting period."

Eventually the presence of Dox became known to Maimone's superiors but he succeeded in convincing them that the dog was exceptional and might prove useful in police operations. Since Maimone pledged himself to cover all upkeep expenses, it was agreed that the dog could remain in the barracks.

"I always treated him with kindness," Maimone recalled. "Never any type of harsh punishment—at worst a slight scolding or a wagging finger of disapproval. A rewarding pat on the head or a tasty *biscotto* [biscuit] for something well done. He returned my affection in full measure. In the beginning and over the years we really got to the point where we could virtually converse together, by signs, tones of voice, barks, etc. You must enter the brain of a dog—think like him. I seldom had to give him orders—he seemed to guess what was the best thing to do or what I deemed was best."

Maimone's first success with his dog in police work occurred in the fall of 1946 at Turin. Patrolling one night with Dox with official approval, Maimone was hurriedly ordered to proceed to a jewelry store, target of a daring robbery. Young Dox seemed to know that something unusual was afoot. He picked up a scent in and near the jewelry store. In less than an hour, tracking on leash, he led Maimone and some other policemen to the robber's hideout. The demonstration was impressive since the route was along much-traversed city streets.

In that same fall Dox and Maimone helped clear up a mystery involving another dog. A man named Argeo Frudua called on local police in the village of Comazzo sull'Adda to help him find his missing canine, a purebred German shepherd. While he was fishing in a forested area near the village his dog had wandered off. Frudua heard a shot in the distance and immediately started whistling for his dog, then searched for him. This search and a subsequent one by the local constabulary proved unavailing. A call to Turin brought Maimone and Dox on the scene.

A black shepherd of the Baltimore police smoothly leaps through a windowlike obstacle.

Attack exercise against a man with a gun.

A view of the kenneling facilities of the Baltimore police.

Man and dog on patrol in Baltimore on a summer day.

Reenactment of an arrest of two lawbreakers in a section of Hartford, Connecticut.

From left to right Dox, Jr., Kira and the fabulous Dox. This photograph was taken when Dox was old and almost blind. Note his damaged left ear.

Dox, Jr., in the countryside outside Rome, Italy. His master, Giovanni Maimone, took this photograph.

Dox, Jr., going over a hurdle at Casa Dox in Rome. Maimone stands in background.

Adam Denholm

Dobermans on night patrol in Macy's New York.

Jerome Ducrot

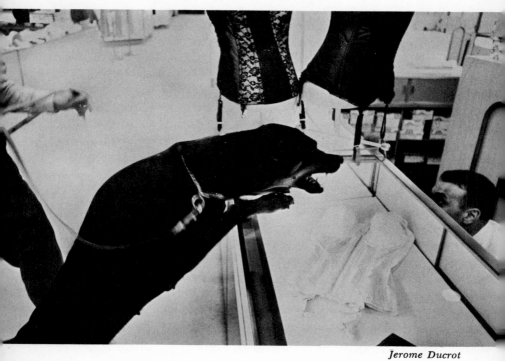

A Doberman of the Canine Corps of Macy's New York in training.

After casting about at the spot where the man had been fishing, the dog of Turin picked up a lead. He soon found the missing dog, lying dead from a gunshot wound in a heavily wooded spot.

Dox was not one for half measures when on the stalk. He began circling farther and picked up another scent. This led to the cottage of a gamekeeper who confessed that he had shot the dog on impulse, fearing he might be attacked by the animal. This was a pretty lame excuse as far as the authorities were concerned and the man was dismissed from his post.

During the remainder of 1946 and in the following year Dox repeatedly proved his worth in pursuit of burglars and in finding missing persons in the environs of Turin and also at more distant points in northern Italy. His know-how increased with each test and the understanding between master and dog in all operations became astounding. One case which involved a skier lost in the mountains drew particular interest in the press. Dox found him, still alive, in the Subiaco area after a posse of human searchers had failed in their quest. Gradually the name of the dog was becoming known throughout Italy and any articles on him and Maimone in newspapers and magazines were sure-fire eye-catchers.

In 1948 Maimone was sent to Sicily in one of those shifts which occur frequently in the police world. The dog went with him. Maimone would escape death by a whisker in the dangerous work impending in Sicily, where gangsterism of various types has flourished for centuries, and where the secret Mafia was born.

The Italian government in the spring of the following year decided the time had come for a major campaign against the Sicilian bandit Salvatore Giuliano. Salvatore, a ruthless outlaw who hardly merited the nickname "Sicilian Robin Hood" bestowed on him by the public, and his band had been terrorizing the land for months. A massive police campaign got under way in the summer of 1949 and eventually proved successful.

By this time Maimone was generally known as "the Hercules Cop" because in a bit of horseplay in Turin he had lifted his commanding officer, weighing some 180 pounds, over his head with one arm. Inevitably, some imaginative reporter, covering the Sicilian "theater of war," suggested that it would be highly romantic for Maimone and Giuliano to meet in a man-to-man gunfight. Maimone said he was quite willing and Giuliano in a letter to Palermo's biggest newspaper announced he was quite ready for such a donnybrook.

The campaign was centered in the Partinico area where the Giuliano gang operated. Dox and his master were in action in the summer and fall of 1949, usually part of heavily armed posses. The bandits did not relish the presence of Dox in their home grounds. They knew that the dog already was credited with some 60 arrests, a number of them effected in minor missions in Sicily. It was a common saying among the outlaws: "You can fight the police but not Dox."

Instructions were given to the Giuliano men to try to kill the dog if possible, with a financial reward awaiting the killer or killers.

One day Dox was unleashed by Maimone, who was accompanied by other policemen, and left to his own devices in the countryside near Montelepre. In this case Dox strayed rather far from the posse and passed near a bush where a bandit was hidden. The outlaw immediately opened fire and hit the dog. He saw Dox roll over and collapse prone on the ground. Believing his shot had been fatal, the bandit took off at a fast pace.

Dox was hit but far from dead. Maimone had taught him how to sham death under certain circumstances, notably when gunplay was involved. The dog was aware that his attacker left the bush and lay still until the bandit had disappeared over a nearby hillock. Then he rose painfully—his hind right paw had been fractured by one of the bullets fired by the man.

He began to trail the bandit, advancing on three legs since the wounded leg was practically useless.

The dog kept his distance and the man never realized that he was being followed. Although wounded, Dox moved faster than his quarry and cannily angling his direction he passed him at a point about six miles from the scene of the attack. Then he hid in a bush alongside a path which the man was following. As soon as the man was opposite his lair, Dox was on him with a fearful roar, fangs bared, eyes blazing. Before the startled outlaw knew what had happened, Dox had his right ankle in his teeth and with a mighty twist had hurled him to the ground, screaming in pain and terror. In his tumble his gun had fallen to the ground, out of reach.

Dox retained his hold on the ankle of the man without deepening it, in line with his training. A few growls and head shakes by the canine nemesis soon brought an end to the man's frantic struggles to release himself. Only then did Dox relinquish his iron grip. A snarl a few inches from his face convinced the bandit that lying quite still on the ground was best for his health.

Then Dox crouched nearby, his eyes fastened on his victim. The man's slightest movement was frozen by a menacing snarl. Guided by an occasional mournful howl from the dog, Maimone and the other policemen came on the spot at dusk. The bandit was still on the ground, Dox watching him, motionless, eyes unwavering. While one policeman handcuffed the bandit, Maimone gave prompt first aid to his injured canine. First aid also was given the wounded man and then both were helped to a nearby highway. Here a police car was available and the injured were taken to a nearby town for medical treatment. Both the man, who was jailed, and the dog recovered from their wounds. Dox's wound was a bad one, however, and despite expert veterinary care he was not fully healed until late in 1949. A far more terrible occurrence was impending for master and dog.

On patrol in the late evening in the month of January, 1950, in the vicinity of Monte Sparagio, Maimone spotted a cave in a hillside and decided to investigate. Dox had been unleashed roaming through bushes and rocks about sixty yards ahead of the policeman.

Automatic in hand—one took no chances in this neck of the woods—Maimone stealthily approached the cave. He halted briefly a few feet from the opening but hearing no sounds from within, entered the cave. It was a grave mistake. Inside were Giuliano himself and three other thugs.

A blast of fire greeted Maimone. He sought to fire back but his automatic jammed. One man rushed up and planted the barrel of a submachine gun in his stomach. Already hit a number of times, half-dazed, the Hercules Cop succeeded in knocking him down with a blow to the head with his automatic before the bandit could pull the trigger. It was hopeless, however. Giuliano and the others continued blasting away and Maimone went down, hit by a total of 27 bullets, four of them in his stomach. The four killers then fled the cave, heading on the run for a small car parked on a nearby roadway, satisfied the target of their planned ambush was finished.

How Dox reacted will never be fully known since in a matter of seconds his master was cut down and lapsed into semi- or complete unconsciousness. Undoubtedly the dog rushed back toward his master but may have lost a few minutes locating him. Perhaps he never saw the fleeing bandits who wasted no time in their getaway. He found the cave, however, and Maimone on the ground, blood oozing from his many wounds. It is believed that the man was completely unconscious at the time. Probably Dox licked his face and barked but his master did not stir or speak. Dox had never coped with such a situation before. But he knew what to do—perhaps as a result of some phase of his training or sheer intelligent reaction. He did not crouch by his master or attempt to chase the killers. Instead he hurried off to seek aid from other humans in the town where he and Maimone were stationed at the time, a relatively short distance from the cave.

The arrival of the lone dog, who made straight for his quarters, was immediately noted by the police, all of whom knew Dox by sight. His barks and excited movements convinced them that something grave had happened. When the dog headed back for the countryside, stopping occasionally and looking back pleadingly, policemen followed him and he guided them to the cave.

Maimone was hurriedly transported for preliminary medical attention to the town and then sent to Palermo's main hospital. For a time doctors despaired of his pulling through but Giovanni was a tough bird. He did. It took three months.

During this time Dox was faithfully nearby day and night. He was permitted to remain on a terrace outside the window of Maimone's room but officially forbidden to enter it or other areas inside the building. Nurses winked at this regulation, however, and permitted him to enter and be close to his master whenever doctors or inspectors were not around. They also saw to it that he was fed at least once a day.

The episode was widely reported in the press and letters of sympathy and gifts addressed to Maimone poured into the hospital, hundreds of them from youngsters throughout Italy.

This marked the end of the "duel" between the man-dog team and Giuliano. The so-called Robin Hood eventually came to a violent end at the hands of a male relative, allegedly greedy for financial rewards promised by the police for the capture or slaying of the bandit.

Before Maimone and Dox returned to Turin in 1952 they participated in numerous minor cases, which, however, always revealed the dog's unusual abilities. In Palermo in 1951 the canine unerringly led police to the hideout of an elusive gang of robbers after police found a handkerchief which one of the thieves had dropped in a raid. The man scent on the handkerchief was more than a month old! In another case Dox found a gold watch which had been stolen from a woman on a beach near Palermo. Dox led Maimone to a nearby bar frequented by rather shady juveniles. Twenty-five men were in the bar but Dox singled out the right one. The watch was in his pocket and he was arrested.

The new stint in Turin would last about five years with master and dog involved in many operations which increased the dog's fame. One is particularly noteworthy since it showed—as in the case of the lost skier—that the presence of snow was no extraordinary hurdle for the Doxian nose.

One evening a woman appeared in tears at the Turin Squadra Mobile headquarters. While she was walking near the Stura Bridge earlier in the day during a snowstorm, her purse had slipped from her hands but she did not perceive this until she had walked on for a considerable distance. It contained a large sum in lire and important documents. She retraced her steps and searched fruitlessly. Then she remembered stories about Dox and headed for the Squadra Mobile and Maimone.

"Sara trovato se non e stato rubato," Maimone told her confidently—"It will be found if it has not been stolen."

The policeman, his dog and the woman proceeded to the area where she believed she had lost the purse. The storm had been fairly heavy and the area was blanketed with snow. Dox sniffed here, sniffed there, and in about ten minutes found the purse under a particularly deep layer of snow.

During these years Dox and Maimone repeatedly participated in police dog contests in Italy. Dox always won and amazed all onlookers. Blindfolded, he infallibly found tiny objects hidden in the contest field or nearby, located the "bodies" of "murdered" persons, and got on the trail of "missing children." Such tests as hurdling obstacles or climbing over them, nailing a "suspect," attacking an armed man, and jumping through flaming hoops were handled with Doxian ease and skill.

An unfortunate incident occurred during a competition before hundreds of onlookers at the town of Acqui. One of the toughest tests involved a passage over a plank a few inches in width and about 17 yards long fastened to the tops of two special frameworks. The aerial bridge was about 15 feet above the ground. Competing canines were called upon to cross the bridge blindfolded. Before Dox's turn several dogs almost made it but fell off either halfway across or near the other end. They were not injured since they fell into big bales of hay. Others just refused to start. When it was his turn, Dox took off gingerly but confidently, blindfolded as the others had been. As he passed the middle point the whole bridge gave way and Dox and the plank crashed to the ground. The plank had been faultily fastened at one end by a careless workman.

In his fall, an awkward one, Dox suffered a bad ankle sprain. Limping painfully, he rose and returned to the base of one of the frameworks and clearly indicated that he would like to try it again. By this time Maimone and a veterinary on the scene had rushed up and the veterinary applied a splint and bandage to the injured limb. Maimone wanted to withdraw the dog from competition but Dox thought otherwise and made this very clear to his master by stubbornly refusing to be led away. Maimone relented. A carpenter securely refastened the plank, and the eye bandage, which had been removed, was put on again. Then Dox climbed up, still limping, and gingerly moved out across the plank. He negotiated it without a serious wobble and descended at the other end amid thunderous cheers from many onlookers. There was no question which dog had won the meet since Dox already led the field in all other tests.

Dox won hands down in a big international police dog contest at Genoa, Italy, in February, 1953. His competitors included crack police dogs from Italy and other European countries. Representatives of practically every important police department in the world were on hand to witness the severe tests involved. All came away amazed over Dox's performances. Umpires unanimously agreed that henceforth he should be considered in a class by himself, "hors concours"—beyond competition.

"As regards the Genoa competition even Maimone—who is a modest man—admits that Dox was sensational," my Rome correspondent wrote me late in 1965 after a visit to the Casa Dox in the Via Cassia on the outskirts of Rome where Maimone now lives and works. "I asked him whether Dox ever participated in other international tournaments. He said 'Si' but added that Dox always ended up by being eliminated in the preliminary trials. This may seem a bit incredible but this is what happened. There was a double barrier one meter [39.37 inches] in height with nails sticking out on top. Each dog had to jump over these barriers to qualify for the finals. Of course something one meter high was nothing for Dox to jump over. However, Dox had been taught to do things in a practical way. Apparently this obstacle aroused his scorn or he felt it was just a waste of time to tackle it. In any case, Dox would trot up to the first barrier, rake it scornfully with his bushy tail, do the same to the second barrier, seeming to say to hell with all this, and trot back to Maimone.

" 'You see, Signora,' Maimone commented with a chuckle, 'he knew he was the greatest dog in the world and he did not have to prove it to himself. It meant elimination from such contests but neither one of us really cared and no doubt the other handlers and their dogs were happy about it!' "

Maimone retired from the police in 1961 in anger over the shabby treatment ultimately accorded him and his aging dog by the Rome authorities.

"On leaving the police he founded Casa Dox," Mrs. Zammarano wrote me. "It is a modest dwelling and here the veteran policeman, who owns some ground around his little house, trains dogs for private clients or sells fine specimens to persons who want to own good animals. He is small but muscular, his face weather-beaten and swarthy. His hair is gray now. Although close to fifty, his movements are brisk and his general appearance vigorous and strong, that of a man in good athletic condition. His whole build denotes unusual physical strength. Maimone's manner is quiet and unassuming, his conversation punctuated by engaging smiles or laughter. He has suffered from a speech defect during recent years which makes it rather hard to understand him but this did not in any way mar our discussion as we sat in his office or toured the kennels.

"Maimone confirmed the fact that Dox could execute one operation which amazed police or any others who witnessed it, probably the only dog in the world who could do it. It took eight years of practice for him to perfect it. He could dismantle a loaded pistol without firing it. With his paws and teeth, he gingerly would remove the clip, after nudging the safety catch into position. Dox also was one of the few dogs in Europe who could untie a person from a chair no matter how complicated or tight the knots.

" 'Oh, you know, Il Vecchio [The Old One] as I used to call him when he really was old, could be really very, very savage when it was called for,' Maimone told me. 'No policeman could desire more aggressiveness. However, I never had any trouble with him when decent people were involved. He seemed instinctively to know who was bad and who was good. As regards children, Signora, he was like butter in their hands. They could mount him like a horse, tweeze his ears, hang onto his tail, ruffle his fur, even tie him with ropes and hoot and whistle all around him. He just took it all good-naturedly. I should point out, too, that in all our years together he never, not on one single occasion, disobeyed an order of mine except on a few days during training when he was very young and sometimes became confused.' "

As in Sicily, Dox did not always escape unscathed in his operations against the lawless. From 1952 to 1961 in Turin and Rome he was hit by bullets fired by fugitives. Fortunately the wounds were not too serious and he was not long out of action. One bullet, however, almost ripped off his left ear and from that time onward it drooped badly, an injury clearly visible in virtually all photographs of the famous dog. In some operations before and after 1952 he was alternately clubbed, kicked or struck with stones. Such resistance to pursuit was futile; in each case Dox kept right on coming and got his quarry.

The dog was destined to gain his greatest fame along with Maimone in Rome, the "Eternal City" where according to legend Romulus and Remus were suckled by a wolf.

In 1957 Maimone and Dox bade farewell to Turin and headed south by train for the capital. Turin authorities had bowed to requests from the Rome police that the now nationally famous team be attached to the capital's police force to help cope with mounting crime problems.

Both were duly enrolled in Rome and attached to the Squadra Mobile. Maimone, a brigadiere at this time, and Dox were assigned to a room in the squad's barracks overlooking the Tiber. Dox was given the rank of corporal, receiving a monthly salary of 28,000 lire (about $48) to be used for the dog's upkeep and medical care.

Their arrival in Rome was reported in the press and the sight of Maimone and Dox on patrol, either on foot or in a car, became a fairly familiar one. To the *buona gente* (good people) this was a pleasurable vision, to the *malviventi* of the capital the source of an uneasiness which would mount steadily during the years to come.

In the ensuing months Maimone and Dox successfully handled a number of minor cases. Their first really impressive accomplishment did not occur until March, 1958—the case of the missing button, recounted earlier in this chapter. Some of the more interesting cases which occurred thereafter, aside from the Donges killing, are worth recording.

On June 11, 1958, a lovely sunny day, Maimone and Dox were patrolling the Trastevere, largely a poor area where the crime graph was high. This was a regular routine for the team, something done more or less on the hunch that Dox's stupendous olfactory organ would pick up the lost trail of some malefactor.

As they rounded a corner on this day, two men on a motorcycle at some distance down the street saw the pair. Without more ado they abandoned the machine and pelted away on foot. Suspicious, Maimone, his dog on leash, hurried up to the machine. Though he had not recognized the two men he let Dox have a good whiff of the motorcycle saddle and the additional seat over the back wheel.

A few sniffs and Dox was off on taut leash; in and out of cramped alleys, up and down dark stairways, across some walls and low rooftops to the door of a dingy top-floor apartment in a tenement. Here Dox stopped and barked. Maimone knocked and a sloppily attired, unkempt woman opened it.

"No, I am the only one here," she replied sullenly in answer to a question from Maimone.

The sergeant and the corporal were not satisfied. Lunging ahead, Dox entered the room and started barking furiously at a sagging sofa in a far corner. Maimone ordered whoever was hidden there to come out, hands first. A man crawled out and then stood up docilely before Maimone, obviously very frightened.

"It might have been the end of me right then and there but for Dox," Maimone told police later in reporting the incident. "While I was questioning the sofa man, another man crept out of a closet and jumped toward me, knife in hand, ready to plunge it into my back. He never made it. Dox sprang on him like a projectile, bowled him over and pinned him down, teeth firmly clamped on the wrist of his knife hand."

Both men were put under arrest by Maimone without further trouble, after confessing they had been the pair on the motorcycle, a stolen machine. Further questioning before imprisonment revealed that both had been involved in a series of burglaries and that the tenement was a clearinghouse for all types of jewel robbers.

Giuseppe Campagna was a respectable minor shopowner in one of Rome's outlying districts. He was a happy family man who had no enemies as far as was known. Returning home one winter's night in 1958, his pocketbook bulging with lire from the day's sales, he was suddenly attacked as he climbed the poorly lit stairs to his apartment. Savagely beaten about the head, he collapsed dying on the stairs. The attack had been so swift that he had not even cried out. Other residents of the building, either ascending the stairs returning from work or descending them to execute some errands, saw the body huddled in a dark corner and immediately notified the police. A local policeman appeared on the scene and in a quick search certified that the attacker, or attackers, had robbed Campagna. His wallet had vanished. The policeman then called in the Squadra Mobile from Rome and men of this unit, including Maimone and his inseparable Dox, hurried to the house.

Without wasting time in questioning members of Campagna's family or other residents of the area for possible clues, Maimone put Dox to work. Campagna had undoubtedly been hit at close quarters, his assailant probably wielding a short club of some kind, and his clothes had been rifled. Dox smelled the man's bloody head and his clothes and then was off on a trail, followed by Maimone and two other policemen. Traversing a rather sparsely populated area near the scene of the crime, he led them to a small bar where some 30 male customers were

gathered. This was known to be a rendezvous for tough charac-
ters in the vicinity. When Maimone entered with Dox and his
companions and asked them whether they knew anything about
the killing, they unanimously denied any knowledge of it. One
of them in fact stepped forward and identifying himself as Agostino Fiorenza, told Maimone he was "a dear friend" of the dead
man and was ready to help the police in capturing the culprit.

While all this was going on, Dox was pulling Maimone this
way and that, smelling industriously at legs and arms. The
"dear friend" had barely made his offer of help when the corporal made his final choice with a loud bark and unwavering
eyes. The eyes were on Agostino Fiorenza. Arrested, he soon
confessed to the crime. The motive was robbery. He had
wielded a hammer. Virtually all of the stolen money was turned
over to the family. For Fiorenza it was a life sentence, the punishment meted out for this type of crime in Italy, which does
not have capital punishment.

In the fall of 1959 the sleuthing duo wrapped up an extortion
plot against Italy's Undersecretary of Foreign Affairs, Carmine
de Martino. The government official received the following
note and instantly reported it to the police:

If you value your skin and that of your children, deliver to the
place indicated on this sheet the sum of five million lire [$8,000] on
Friday, August 28, at 23 hours [11 P.M.] in a package camouflaged
with lettuce leaves. Do not notify newspapers or the police; otherwise it will be bad for you; when you least expect it, I will blow up
your home.

The money was to be placed in a tree on the Via Annia
Regilla, according to indication made on the letter by the
writer. The tree was in a flat field alongside the road, its position clearly shown.

A few days before the deadline, Squadra Mobile agents,
dressed as garbage men, dug a large hole and constructed a

makeshift cover camouflaged with rubbish. The police were relying on Dox. The dog had thoroughly sniffed the letter, which was turned over to the police immediately without too much handling by various persons.

On the night of August 28, Maimone and the dog lay in wait. For hours nobody showed up; then, just before sunrise, Dox who knew when to keep his mouth shut, nudged Maimone, who was fighting off sleep and was somewhat chilled by the night air by this time. From a peephole Maimone saw a shadowy figure near the tree which was being watched. He loosed Dox and he was off in a blur of speed. Before the man realized what was happening Dox had knocked him to the ground with a flying leap and had him nailed, bared fangs within inches of his face. Maimone had no trouble in making the arrest. The man screamed, "I confess everything—call the dog off!"

De Martino's financial reward to Dox and Maimone was an extremely generous one.

During his career Dox did not tangle only with men. A woman was the central figure in a drama that occurred in November, 1959, one that perhaps garnered more headlines for the dog and Maimone than any other.

Valeria Menconi, thirty-four, was a comely girl endowed with above-average intelligence and an eye for elegant clothes. Valeria, once an outstanding law student at the University of Rome, had, by dint of hard work, attained the rank of chief secretary to the vice-mayor in the capital's City Hall. In 1959 she was engaged to be married, deeply in love with her fiancé, a good-looking young Roman named Sergio Marini.

In the fall of that year, Sergio became one of 2,500 candidates for civil service exams applying to 200 openings for public notaries, positions which in Italy provide a fairly comfortable income. Valeria decided she could help her lover in his ambitions.

Through some bureaucratic hocus-pocus, Valeria managed to

get her hands on the daily set of answers to the three-day examination. During the first test, she delivered the keyed answers in person to the exam-room proctor who, in turn, for 600,000 lire (about $1,000) had agreed to slip them to Marini. She did the same thing the second day, but by this time, an anonymous phone call had already tipped off the police that the answers were leaking out through the medium of a City Hall secretary.

Squadra Mobile put a secret watch on the woman and, on the third day, while on her way to deliver the last set of answers to the proctor, Valeria became suspicious that she was being followed. With the damning evidence of the exam answers tucked in a small change purse, she knew she had to work fast.

Attempting to throw the police off, she followed a confusing path among twisting streets to the Testaccio Bridge, which crossed the Tiber River near St. Peter's. There, she suddenly staged a fainting spell near one of the parapets. In the process of swooning to the ground, she deftly let the change purse with the papers in it fall unobserved into the water.

Stalking detectives were near and at this juncture approached the woman and helped her rise from the ground. Valeria played out her role, telling them she frequently suffered from dizziness and fainting spells. The police, however, took her to headquarters for an interrogation. Here Valeria insisted she was innocent of involvement in any fraud connected with the examinations. Aware that the police had not perceived her sly maneuver with the papers at the bridge, she willingly let them rummage in her larger purse which had contained the change purse. This revealed nothing incriminating, neither did a quick frisking of her clothes by a woman official.

The police were convinced, however, that she was guilty and had somehow got rid of the evidence. But where and how? The police had to move rapidly. This might be something for the great Dox. The team was called in.

At police headquarters, Il Gigante, accompanied by his master, gave Valeria's feet and hands a good sniffing. Then Maimone, other policemen and the dog headed for the Testaccio Bridge zone. Police believed that Valeria had done some sleight of hand in that sector and had decided further investigation should start there. A cursory search near the spot where she had fallen at the time she was taken into custody, however, had not yielded any clues.

Arrived at the bridge, Dox first sniffed at the spot where Valeria was seized and then began casting about, with occasional helpful promptings from his stocky master. This quest led the dog and Maimone to the parapets under the bridge and beyond them. In less than half an hour, the dog had found the missing purse. As a result of the current it had become partially lodged under a half inch of riverbank sand some 300 yards distant from the bridge. The feat was an exceptional one since a water-borne object can almost never be traced by a dog.

Faced with the incriminating evidence, Valeria tearfully confessed everything. The solution of the case resulted in blaring headlines. Four arrests were made and the whole examination declared null and void. Valeria's career at City Hall was finished and so were Marini's hopes of ever becoming a notary public.

A collie puppy was the "quarry" in a touching episode which had a happy ending, thanks to Il Gigante.

Gisa Nanni, a Roman woman of the poorer strata, her husband an unemployed bricklayer, had been informed by her doctor that she would have to undergo a serious operation in February, 1960. The Nannis, who had a young son named Elio, were at wit's end how to pay for this, no reserve funds being available. Her husband appealed to a sister living in France for some aid. The sister wrote back that she did not have money to spare but that she was shipping them by train a collie puppy which had been presented to her by a friend. The puppy had an excellent pedigree and they could sell him in Italy for a good price to meet the cost of the operation.

The pup, a beautiful animal, was delivered safe and sound at the Nanni home. The dog was well treated while the unemployed father began to make inquiries regarding a possible purchaser. One morning Elio took the puppy for a walk. He soon returned home and tearfully told his mother that he had lost the dog in the vicinity of the Via del Carso.

Signor Nanni promptly called the police and Dox and Maimone were on another hunt. After smelling the boy and a blanket on which the puppy had slept or rested, Dox got a good scent. Then he and Maimone were led by the boy to the area where Elio had first missed the pup. Despite the fact that it was raining, Dox's nose did not fail. It was a very long trail, however; he found the pup, shivering and frightened, crouching behind some garbage cans at the base of a building in the Capannelle area. The bewildered pup, who had kept on going in a more or less definite direction when he left Elio, was found some 13 miles from the point where he had first disappeared.

He was immediately brought back to the Nanni home. Maimone, a man of kindly disposition, reached into his own pockets and provided the harried family with some helping funds. Things went all right from then on for the family. Newspapers delighted in the story, so did their readers, a purchaser soon materialized and the pup was sold for an excellent price.

In 1960 Dox, acting on his own initiative, saved a six-year-old girl from being run over by an automobile. Dox and Maimone were on a leisurely patrol in the Via Lungotevere Marzio when an automobile came roaring down the street, going much too fast. It headed straight for the girl who was playing with a ball in the street. Before Maimone knew what was afoot Dox apparently realized that only lightning action could save the youngster. In a mighty heave and bound which ripped the leash from his master's hand, the dog headed for the girl and tumbled her out of the path of the car. The speed demon at the wheel missed them by inches.

The sterling service of Dox and Maimone in law enforcement work came to an end in 1961 in a melancholy manner, with little governmental gratitude for past service in evidence.

In January of that year Maimone had two dogs at the Squadra Mobile barracks, Dox and another Alsatian of good pedigree he had purchased the previous year and had named Dox II. On January 15 Maimone was bluntly informed by top echelons that the two dogs had been dismissed from service as of that day. Maimone's protests and requests for an explanation of the action were so much wasted breath. Newspapers stated later that the decision came from "high up" in the government but names were not mentioned. Assertedly one or several persons had ruled that since neither Dox nor Dox II had been trained at the police dog schools at Nettuno and Monte Mario they had no right to be attached to the police. A preposterous view as far as Dox was concerned, since he unquestionably did not at any time need a degree from the two schools to qualify for any police test.

The whole "conspiracy"—as it was called in some quarters—against Dox has never been fully explained. Possibly envy in some government departments of the public acclaim heaped on Dox and Maimone and the fact that admirers of the dog had given its master monetary donations may have been some of the factors in this development.

The order was not only sudden but cruel—the dogs must be out of the barracks before nightfall January 15 and for good. Maimone's unswerving loyalty to his aging companion and his new canine friend proved to be a shining light in this crisis.

Maimone, a bachelor, had no other home than the barracks. Sadly, he led the two animals out of the barracks area and found them new emergency quarters—if this word is applicable—on a sidewalk along the Tiber. Maimone had chosen the location so that the animals would be partly protected from the biting winter wind. After tying them to a small tree he provided them with two blankets and food. He watched over them as frequently as he could during the night, ransacking his brains on just what his next move should be.

His decision was reached the following day. He resigned from the police force.

News of the dismissal got into the papers the same day, along with pictures of the two canines on the sidewalk. The reaction in the press was an angry one. In the *Domenica del Corriere,* the well-known journalist Indro Montanelli bitterly scored the dismissal action:

Dox always heeded the call of duty, tracking down criminal after criminal. His feats won national and international acclaim . . . thus we all thought that he faced an honorable and comfortable old age, his final years brightened by official gratitude, his name honored. For dogs there are no lifetime senatorial posts but there can be straw pallets and soup or bones. No dog merited gratitude more than Dox. Instead, we now see photographs of Dox and his canine companion lying like beggars, like two pariahs, on a sidewalk along the Tiber.

Almost immediately many offers of aid to the dogs were made by admirers. The noted Italian stage and screen comedian Toto (Antonio di Curtis, a nobleman) and actress Anna Magnani, both great animal lovers, offered immediate asylum in country estates they owned. The upshot was that the two dogs found comfortable quarters in a hotel room, the bill footed by Toto. They remained there a few weeks until Maimone, fulfilling a plan he had toyed with for some time, obtained the property which would become the Casa Dox.

To the credit of police officials, Dox continued to receive his pay of about $48 a month until December 31, 1961. Every month during this period Dox would appear with Maimone at the payment desk at police headquarters where the fifteen-year-old veteran would stand up on his hind legs and place his fore-paws on the desk. The pay was then handed to Maimone.

During his years as a police dog Il Gigante was credited with at least 400 arrests in an enormous variety of cases ranging from major to minor. He also was involved in hundreds of episodes in which arrests did not occur, entailing the recovery of lost property, tracing missing children and the like. He won 27 silver medals and four gold ones either in competitive meets or as rewards for distinguished service. Police admitted that during his service in Rome he cracked more cases than any Roman human sleuth did in the same period.

Some months prior to the cashiering, Dox had starred in a film about his life made at Cinécitta near Rome. The movie was a box-office flop, mainly because the Italian producer used none of Dox's real exploits and fictionalized the whole story line. It even included a silly boy-and-dog-meet-girl sequence which had no place in such a production.

Maimone received $10,000 for this which he placed in a bank as a sort of social security for Dox. A large part of this sum went into the purchase of the Casa Dox and surrounding property.

One of the blights of great age inevitably hit Dox in his last years. By 1960, while still operating with the police, a cataract had brought blindness to his right eye. In 1962 the motion picture firm of Buffardi contacted Maimone at Casa Dox seeking an old trained dog who could play dead and perform in various other ways in a film entitled *Il Smemorato* (The Forgotten Man). It was agreed that Dox would do well and soon he and Maimone were on location.

One of the acts called for the aged dog to jump over a chair blocking a doorway. This Dox did smoothly several times. The reel completed, the chair was removed from the doorway. Trotting ahead of Maimone in leaving the room through the same door, Dox jumped again as if the chair were still there.

Maimone knew about the trouble with the right eye but now realized that his pet was also virtually blind in the left eye, that he was operating almost entirely by smell and hearing. Nonetheless Dox fulfilled his role in the picture faultlessly. None except Maimone realized how gravely handicapped the dog was.

The famous dog was not mated with any female until late in life, since it was one of Maimone's theories that sexual activity tended to lessen a dog's effectiveness as far as police operations were concerned.

The sergeant relented, however, in July, 1960, while both were still in police service. Dox—98 years old by human standards—was mated with a beautiful female Alsatian named Elca, owned by a wealthy Roman. She presented Dox with a litter of five males and four females, their fur unmistakably similar to that of Dox. During puppyhood the dogs were cared for at Casa Dox. Eventually some were presented to the owner of Elca, others were sold to reliable purchasers and two were retained by Maimone. These were a beautiful female named Kira and the most promising male of the litter, honored with the title of Dox, Jr.

Dox, Jr., is very much in evidence today at the Casa Dox, a powerful, intelligent animal, his general appearance somewhat resembling that of Dox.

"Maimone admits that Dox, Jr., is somewhat exceptional but doubts that there ever will be another dog like 'old Dox,'" my Rome correspondent informed me in September, 1965. "According to him, one very great difference is in the attack patterns of father and son. Dox, Sr., always sat on his haunches a moment and gave his prey a chance to defend himself—a gentlemanly gesture but one that earned him his wounds. Dox, Jr., shows no such chivalrous streak but pounces from a distance of about seven yards without any waiting at all. When Maimone with the aid of the elder Dox was training the youngster, Il Gigante was clearly jealous and often would cunningly lead the trainee astray with various tricks. Maimone got quite angry about this and several times threatened to give the father a cuff for his *furberia* [cunning]. He finally cured him by laughing at him and apparently Dox, Sr., realized that he was being ridiculed and just quit playing pranks on his son.

"During the years Maimone repeatedly turned down offers to purchase Dox. One wealthy Frenchman was ready to disburse some $15,000 for the dog in his prime, but the answer was no. It probably was one of the highest prices offered for a dog in all history. 'To give up Dox would have been like selling my own child,' Maimone says.

"I don't think Maimone is actually bitter about his differences with the police but he is definitely displeased with the whole affair. I do not think he is particularly keen on training dogs for police work anymore. His Casa Dox business is going favorably. He trains dogs for private clients and has from 25 to 30 of them 'in residence' most of the time. He has five scrapbooks on hand containing innumerable newspaper and magazine clippings dealing with Dox's exploits."

His beloved master was always near Dox in the dog's declining days. In the last months the dog could neither see nor hear but he always sensed Maimone's presence when he came near and showed his joy with tail thumpings and feeble barks.

The end came peacefully for the canine Sherlock at Casa Dox on June 11, 1965. Maimone was stroking his head and murmuring farewells when he breathed his last. By human count he was 133 years old. He is buried in an unmarked grave on the grounds of Casa Dox but the grilled enclosure in which his kennel is located has been turned into a modest shrine to his memory by Maimone. There is a piece of crepe on the gate and two candles and some framed photographs of Dox are visible in the enclosure.

" 'His time on this earth seemed so short,' Maimone said sadly as we stopped before the shrine in our last interview," Mrs.

Zammarano reported. "You know at one time they planned to place a life-size statue of him in the Borghese Gardens or some other park. He deserved it. But nothing came of it. Let us hope there is some kind of *paradiso* for good dogs!

" 'Ah, for me, you know, there never will be another Dox,' Maimone said shaking his head pensively as he bade me a courteous farewell."

Come, Watson, come! The game is afoot.
—SHERLOCK HOLMES in "The Adventure of the
Abbey Grange," by Sir Arthur Conan Doyle

7

Sleuth of London

THE prospect of violent action seemed generally remote to Police Constable Arthur Holman as he sipped a cup of tea in the Tooting police station on Mitcham Road, southwest London, on Sunday, June 13, 1954.

The tea seemed particularly delicious to Holman in the wake of several hours of tedious patrolling in the rainswept streets of the Mitcham area with Rex III. The rain had kept most of the people indoors. Nothing of any importance had occurred to break the monotony of this morning assignment. Even his faithful Alsatian seemed bored by the morning's regular patrol, his usual high spirits dampened by the downpours.

The only episode worth remembering as far as Holman was concerned involved a verbal exchange with an elderly lady, all on a very polite level. This Englishwoman had strong ideas regarding a double standard for dogs and Englishmen in the matter of rainproof clothing.

Spotting Holman and the Alsatian strolling along a sidewalk, she hurried up in great agitation, umbrella held aloft, and said irritably:

"Your dog will catch his death of cold in this chill rain. You, Constable, are dressed up in a mac and very comfortably protected but what about the poor dog?"

Rex gave the woman a speculative but friendly look as Holman replied with a smile:

"Indeed, madam, your thought is a nice one but do not worry too much. My dog's fur protects him in all kinds of weather and we have often been out for hours in much worse than this. He's young, and fit as a fiddle."

"Oh, yes, I see, but I still don't believe it's quite right, you know," the woman commented. She departed after this statement but gave the constable a parting glance which seemed to imply that she would soon belabor the Royal Society for the Prevention of Cruelty to Animals with some acid comments on treatment accorded dogs by the police.

Holman and his dog, one of the most noted four-footed cops in K-9 annals, had been on duty since 9 A.M. when Holman decided it was time to return to the station for a noontime break. Entering the station, Holman's first action was to give his

wettened dog a thorough drying with a towel, this type of attention always advisable when a dog has been out in the rain.
Then he patted his head and ordered him to lie down inside the
building near the main entrance. There was no necessity to tie
up Rex. Orders from his master were implicitly obeyed by the
dog, an exceptionally fine specimen of German shepherd,
weighing about 80 pounds, its shading black and tan, eyes extremely alert and intelligent.

A quick check at the desk disclosed that no special messages
had come in for the man-dog team and Holman proceeded to
the canteen for some warm refreshment. Munching on a sand-
wich and sipping his tea, Holman mused on the duller moments
of police work; this morning had been just another one. Probably nothing would happen in the hours of scheduled duty
ahead, unless some other old ladies enlivened the patrol, Holman reflected gazing through a rain-splattered window at the
quiet streets below.

Whether the climate was fair or foul, the duty hours exciting
or monotonous, there always was a cheerful prospect for Holman and Rex after their daily stint: the trip back to the modest
but comfortable Holman home in the Mitcham area. Its tenants, Arthur, his pretty wife, Betty, their daughter, Vivienne,
and their son, Richard, were a happy group. It also was a joyous
place for Rex, who was considered and treated like a member of
the family.

By this year the Holman-Rex team was well known in London and elsewhere in England. The dog was considered the top
canine sleuth of the then burgeoning police dog division of the
London Metropolitan Police, which today is the most important in the world with some 200 dogs in operation. In the four
years since Rex had been assigned to Holman, the dog had been
credited with scores of arrests, his name as legendary in England
as that of Dox in Rome.

Holman and Rex were attached to the Tooting police station

at this time, part of W Division of the police No. 4 District, a wide beat embracing most of the Metropolitan area south of the Thames. Although the team was on call anywhere in the No. 4 District, the regular patrols of Holman and Rex centered in the W Division, which included the Mitcham area.

Holman was finishing his repast with a second "cuppa" when a sergeant of the Criminal Investigation Division of Scotland Yard, whom he knew, dropped into the canteen.

"I'm going with a detective-constable to Tynemouth Road to pick up an Army deserter," he told Holman after an exchange of friendly greetings. "Would you like to come and watch the back of the house with Rex in case he tries to make a run for it?"

"By all means," Holman replied.

Holman, the sergeant and another policeman and Rex piled into a patrol car and headed for Tynemouth Road. What transpired is dramatically described in the book Holman wrote about his dog entitled *My Dog Rex*.

When the patrol car drew up in Tynemouth Road I went to the back [of the building] with Rex and waited for something to happen. Usually this type of assignment was a short one. A knock at the door . . . brief introductions and a statement of business . . . a search, followed, perhaps, by a short scuffle . . . a formal caution— and within five minutes of arriving we would be on our way back to the police station.

But on this occasion ten minutes passed without my hearing from my colleagues, and I wondered what was wrong. I did not know the name of the man we were after, or his description, and I assumed that to be on the safe side I would have to stop any male who appeared through the back door. When after twenty minutes, nothing had happened I decided to find out what was causing the delay, and we reached the front of the house just in time to hear shouts and see a man break from the police car and rush round the corner into Ashbourne Road.

Rex was not on leash but he seemed fully aware that action of some type was impending. Tensely he waited for a word of command. A snapped "Stop him" from Holman was enough and Rex was off like a streak in the drizzle.

The dog skidded into Ashbourne Road and as I sprinted after him I saw the deserter turn into Thirsk Road. Still running, the man thrust his hand into the pocket of his raincoat and pulled out a gun. Without slowing down, he half turned, took aim at the dog and fired. Mercifully he missed, and as he pulled the trigger Rex leapt up and sank his teeth into the gunman's right arm. The deserter tried to shake free, and as he moved his arm to do so the revolver was fired a second time.

All this had occurred in less time than it takes to tell. When the second shot was fired I was rounding the corner into Thirsk Road, and my attention was so firmly riveted upon Rex and the gunman that I did not see a low wall projecting from the corner. I tripped over and sprawled headlong on the pavement. The constable, coming up behind me, rushed past and made for the gunman. Rex still had his grip upon the man's arm, and when the constable wavered for a moment, as though afraid of the dog, I promptly called off the Alsatian. I was back on my feet now, and as Rex ran back toward me the gunman saw his chance. He twisted free from the policeman and rushed away down Thirsk Road.

"Stop him!" I called. Rex wheeled in his tracks, flashed past the detective-constable, and bounded after the deserter. Glancing over his shoulder, the man saw the dog coming at him, immediately skidded to a halt, and turned. With brutal deliberation, mouth twisted into a snarl, he levelled the gun, waited until Rex was about to leap, then pushed the revolver into the dog's face, and pulled the trigger.

The force of the explosion spun Rex in a complete circle. He collapsed on the ground and lay there motionless and silent. I felt neither anger nor sorrow. I was too numbed by the dreadful certainty that Rex was dead. How could the man have failed to have shot him straight between the eyes?

By stopping to shoot at the dog the gunman lost a valuable couple of seconds, and the constable was able to grab hold of him again. My immediate concern was for Rex, and as I went toward the dog I saw the gunman struggling grimly with the detective. Before I reached Rex, however, and to my amazement and joy, the Alsatian suddenly trembled, raised his head, and climbed to his feet. It was obvious that he was dazed and could not see, yet such was his courage he began to stagger toward the sound of the scuffle.

"Down, Rex! Down!" I shouted. I knelt beside him and saw that the bullet had grazed his left ear and that his eyes were blinded by the white spots of powder burns. Without even a whimper, he sat down trying to paw away the pain in his eyes.

Holman then left Rex and helped the other policeman finally subdue the gunman, who was forced into the patrol car. Then Holman helped the dog into the car. Only then did Holman learn details of what had happened when the deserter was accosted in the house. The two policemen had no difficulty in entering the building and the deserter made no attempt to hide or escape. He had acted with deceptive submissiveness and had answered various preliminary questions readily. He denied having any arms in his possession and had consented to go along with the police so that his case could be turned over to army authorities. He had barely entered the car when he made his break, having successfully dulled the alertness of the two policemen.

"What a good job we took you with us this morning!" the C.I.D. man who was at the wheel said. "He'd have got away if it hadn't been for Rex."

The gunman, now under arrest, was turned in at the Tooting police station and Rex and his master were driven immediately to the Holman home for emergency care.

His mind, dominated by "a terrible fear I could not define," Holman gently carried Rex into the house.

I told my wife briefly what had happened, and she stood silently by me as I bathed the Alsatian's eyes and ear with boric acid crystals dissolved in warm water. When, after a while, I realized that Rex was able to see again my strength seemed to surge back, and a cup of tea and a cigarette made me feel more like my old self.

Then Rex was taken to a police veterinary and he told Holman, to his infinite pleasure, that the hurt was fortunately not serious. He said the burn marks would disappear within a few days and that no permanent injury was involved.

Back home Arthur's wife and daughter took turns at bathing the dog's eyes, amid a continual coming and going of reporters anxious for details about another exploit by one of England's favorite dogs.

Rex was scheduled to participate in a police dog meet the next day. After some hesitation, Holman decided that the dog should compete. His sight appeared excellent on the morning after the attack, although there were ugly white spots in his eyes. The pain seemed to have gone and he was as lively as ever.

"The competition did, however, include a gun chase and I wondered whether it was advisable to subject Rex to this type of ordeal so soon after the 'real life' shooting," Holman wrote. "I debated the problem and decided not to eliminate Rex from the gun chase; it would enable me to see whether the dog's nerve had been affected by the experience."

Nothing like it. In spite of blank cartridges fired at close range by a "fugitive," Rex bored in without faltering. If anything, the previous day's encounter made him more savage and the "fugitive's" padded attack clothing was given a fearful mauling. Holman was so proud of his dog that he lifted him in his arms and gleefully carried him off the field.

All three policemen involved in the arrest of the gunman

received monetary rewards of fifteen pounds each from the Bow Street Reward Fund. In an impressive ceremony at the Tooting station Rex, already the recipient of many decorations and awards, received two more, a police silver medal for bravery and the bronze medal of the National Canine Defence League.

The gunman got what was coming to him in Old Bailey court. Twelve years' imprisonment.

Fan mail from young and old, from all parts of England, flowed into the Holman residence addressed to Rex. One lady mailed in a medallion for Rex bearing the figure of St. Francis which she said had been specially blessed for her by her parish priest. Residents of Mitcham contributed to the stamping of a special medal bearing the legend: *To Rex III for courage and devotion to duty.*

This hubbub over Rex was nothing new to the Holmans, since the dog was assigned to Arthur in 1950 in the early phase of Scotland Yard's police dog operations. In April, 1951, Rex III, the famous Labrador Ben, and six other dogs of the force, Dante, Earl, Rap, Blaze, Rajah and Rex II,* had gone through their paces in a Command Performance in the presence of Britain's sovereigns. This was the highest possible tribute as far as England was concerned to the usefulness of police dogs.

All the dogs performed well in various tests including attacks on "gunmen" and spectacular obedience and tracking tests. Rex III and Ben gave the most outstanding demonstrations, as was generally expected.

After the exhibition King George VI and Queen Elizabeth expressed a wish to meet the handlers and their dogs, the teams standing in line at attention.

---

* No relation of Rex III. The name Rex is a popular one for dogs both among police and civilians in England and many police dogs are given this name in that country.

The sovereigns spoke graciously with each trainer in turn and occasionally stopped and lightly petted some of the dogs, including Rex.

For Holman the Queen had a question with a naturally feminine slant:

"How does your wife like having a police dog at home?"

"My wife is very fond of the dog, Your Majesty," Holman replied. "He is an excellent fellow, really a member of the family, Your Majesty."

"And how does the dog get on with your children?" the Queen then asked.

"Extremely well, Your Majesty," the constable replied.

The Queen smiled and moved on and King George said to Holman, "You have a very good-looking dog. I shouldn't like him after me."

Fortunately, this time there was no flare-up between Ben and Rex III. Just as in the case of some humans, there was friction between the noted black dog and Rex. Only on two occasions during his police career did Rex disobey a clear-cut order from Holman—and Ben was involved in both instances.

Ben had gained fame before Rex. He was one of the first dogs trained by Scotland Yard when it seriously undertook K-9 operations in 1946 after World War II. The first flare-up between him and Rex occurred during a police dog demonstration in the London area in 1950—with Holman and Ben's master, Police Constable Herbert Shelton, present. Holman's implicit faith in Rex's obedience under all circumstances was actually to blame. There are some situations which are just too much for even the best-trained canine.

Both Shelton and Holman were good friends and it was agreed on this occasion that Holman would act as a fugitive and that the black Labrador would go after him. Holman told Rex to "sit," which the dog did. As an extra precaution he put him on leash and handed it to another policeman present to hold while he made his getaway.

Holman started running with Ben after him, barking loudly. The sight galvanized Rex. He broke free and in split seconds the two dogs were at it hammer and tongs, slashing and snarling at each other. Shelton and Holman soon separated them but damage had been achieved, although not serious. Ben had a scratched nose and one of Rex's ears was cut.

The two dogs did not clash again for three years; however, enmity and a memory of the fight had not vanished.

In 1953 both dogs were again competing with other canines in a display put on for visiting officers of the French Navy.

During obedience tests the dogs formed one line and the handlers another, men and dogs facing each other over a distance of some 40 yards. Rex was next to Ben and opposite them stood Shelton and Holman. Holman called Rex to him when it was the turn of this team to demonstrate obedient cooperation. As Rex rose to obey, Ben gave him a sidelong snarl. Rex forgot all about his master's order and went after the Labrador with enthusiasm. Although a Labrador is often considered a better fighter than an Alsatian, Holman claimed that Rex got the best of this encounter before they were separated by their two handlers. Ben's handsome face was bleeding from various scars while Rex had not received a scratch. Both dogs were punished with a scolding which obviously proved a lasting admonition. They never tangled again although they were competitors in other ensuing meets.

Like all the other dog handlers of the British police, Holman had excellent qualifications for this type of work, including the all-important factor, a long-standing love of dogs. He was born in 1911 in the small Berkshire village of Theale. Throughout his youthful years there was virtually no period when he did not own some kind of dog. After leaving school at fourteen some of his first jobs were with dogs, going out with sheep and cattle dogs owned by local farmers.

In May of 1932 he joined the Metropolitan Police force and remained in London with the force during World War II. After the war he was attached to the C.I.D. as an aide to the Ghost Squad, carrying out undercover investigations in the Tooting, Balham and Mitcham areas. During the thirties he married a girl with whom he had gone to school, his present wife, Betty.

When Scotland Yard decided to expand its dog operations in 1950 Holman was one of several men who volunteered for such duty, and was accepted.

When he and two other policemen reported at Imber Court to pick the dogs they liked, Holman chose Rex, then about a year old, and was formally assigned to this dog. Holman recalled:

It was my 39th birthday and I really could not have had a better present. As soon as I saw him I knew I had not made a mistake. To people who have never owned an animal a dog is simply a dog; there is no adjectival qualification or distinction. All the descriptive poetry in the world could not convey to them how I felt at that moment—the thrill of tingling excitement that went through me when I saw that Rex was indeed a king among dogs. An Alsatian, big for his 12 months, with black-and-tan markings, clear brown eyes and sharply defined, intelligent features, he had a vital force I have never known in another dog, before or since.

Rex, who had a good pedigree, had served in previous months as a guard-companion to the night watchman at the French Legation in London. Automation caused a change in his career and marked the start of his adventurous days with Holman. Automatic burglar alarms were installed in the Legation and Rex was presented to the Metropolitan Police for use in law enforcement.

"That dog is going to be a cracker!" an expert dog handler

named Tom Scott told Holman after the choice had been made. The forecast was destined to be splendidly fulfilled.

A minor uproar occurred at the Holman home when Arthur arrived with Rex—for that was where the dog would reside, as is generally the case with Metropolitan Police. Betty exclaimed, "I expected a Labrador," daughter Vivienne, then ten years old, grumbled, "I wanted a newborn puppy!" and son Richard, fourteen, mumbled, "I don't think much of that!" A curt "Police orders" from Holman quelled all such opposition.

There followed weeks of patient training to prepare the dog for the rigorous tests ahead in the dangerous world of law enforcement. Rex was highly intelligent but as with all canines the more complex phases of dog obedience were not completed without many vexing failures.

Fortunately, handlers were permitted a great deal of freedom in training their dogs, making for highly personalized teamwork.

"This was as it should be, for every dog has its own personality and I do not believe that the best standard can be obtained from classes of mass instruction," Holman wrote, his view coinciding with one frequently expressed by the master of Rome's Dox.

Holman cleverly evolved his own particular command words and soon taught Rex to obey only his voice except for some minor orders given at home by members of the Holman family.

My work would have been wasted if Rex obeyed other people's commands. If, for instance, I told Rex to stop a criminal, yet he took notice when the prisoner, knowing the jargon, said "Leave . . . Sit" we would be faced with a situation bordering on the farcical. So I trained him to obey only my voice by administering a verbal rebuke when he took heed of anyone else's. To help avoid confusion if there was more than one handler and dog around, I also changed the words of commands. Thus I would say "Hand" while other handlers employed "Come!" Rex not understanding the latter word, would take no notice, even though he might have muddled our voices.

Teaching Rex not to stray off and come back immediately to his handler's side was a tough instructional phase—nothing new in police dog training. During a freak snowstorm in April of 1950 Rex, whose lead (the English word for leash) had been removed, strayed off with a vengeance. Half-frozen and deeply irritated, Holman struggled after him in open terrain for an hour before he got him back.

The next day the performance was repeated, Holman vainly trying to lure him back with pieces of meat. When it happened for the third time Holman devised a maneuver which is a useful tip to dog trainers. He would use a mild form of "artillery" against the rover.

As a boy Holman had been a crack shot with a catapult and he now secured one and some special ammunition—acorns. When Rex again began wandering, heedless of the shouted "Hand," his master let fly, the acorn hitting the tip of the dog's ear. No other shot was necessary. Rex, who was some distance away, was so surprised at the fact that Arthur could thus flick him that he trotted back immediately. From then on the order "Hand" was no source of trouble, although the affrays with Ben might be considered exceptions.

Holman also has some good advice for dog owners in general.

No dog worthy of his biscuits likes to be on a lead, and I always put the lead out of sight when calling Rex. I did not want him to think he was going to lose his freedom by obeying my order. I know there is nothing more infuriating than to call a dog and not to have him come, and although your instinct might be to beat the dog for his disobedience, I believe strongly that this is a monstrous injustice to the animal. Dogs cannot reason as we do and from his point of view he is being punished for coming to you—for obeying your order. When the dog ultimately comes he should be fussed over. He will grow to believe that you are calling him to pet him and the chances are that soon he will come quickly whenever you tell him to. I feel, too, that it is cruel to the dog to have him tugging at the end of a lead which is pulling against his windpipe. Far better, surely, to train the dog to walk to "Heel."

One of the most important commands in the whole obedience repertoire was the simple shout "NO!" which could be used in all kinds of situations. It is especially vital in chasing criminals to keep a dog on the right track and not be deflected by the presence of other persons.

This was underscored in an episode which involved Rex and his master in later years. One night they were patrolling the Battersea area in a car looking for a thief who had taken part in what in England is known as a "smash and grab" raid, or in more technical language, forcible entry and burglary.

Entering a side street Holman suddenly spotted a running man carrying what appeared to be twelve or fifteen raincoats—obviously something odd about this situation.

Holman promptly shouted, "Stop him!" Rex hurtled through an open window of the car before Holman could open the door. By coincidence another man came hurrying into the street, his course diagonally across that of the man running away with the coats. This confused Rex and he swerved and headed for the new arrival. A shouted "No" from Holman promptly told Rex that he was on the wrong track and the dog then swung off in the right direction. Rex promptly cornered the man with the coats, who was howling for help when Holman came up, Rex snarling menacingly and snapping at his legs and arms. He was one of the thieves involved and was arrested and later given a prison term.

Inevitably, dogs trained to attack do sometimes bite people when it is not called for. One day when Rex, by now a fully trained dog, and Holman were patrolling Mitcham Common, a woman was bitten seriously although it is not certain whether Rex was responsible. On this occasion a big Alsatian, hankering for a fight, made for Rex, heedless of the shouts of his mistress, who came running after him. In seconds both dogs were in a fierce fight. The woman came up shouting "Do something!" and tried to grab her dog. He was too strong for her and Holman finally separated them, the challenger scuttling behind her skirts, tail between his legs.

The melée was over but Holman perceived with shock that the woman was bleeding from an ugly gash in one of her legs, obviously caused by fangs. He immediately offered to find transport for her to a nearby hospital but she declined and hurried away with her dog. Only later did Holman learn that the woman had been forced to spend three weeks in a hospital when the gash became ulcerated. It was impossible to establish, however, which dog had inflicted the wound. In all likelihood it was Rex since the woman was the other dog's mistress. Certainly, it was the result of "battle confusion" and not intended for her at all.

On July 14, 1950, Rex, along with other new dogs who had undergone training, passed final tests and they and their handlers from then on were on duty as teams.

Arduous days, months and years followed in which Arthur and Rex became involved in all types of cases, the dog becoming daily more skillful at whatever problems were involved. Before Rex's career ended he would have 125 arrests to his credit. His record became so outstanding that it was generally agreed that he was the best canine on the force. The order from superiors to "get Holman and that dog from Tooting on this case" cut leisure time for Holman and his companion to a minimum. Summonses wakening Holman from deep slumber in early morning hours and hurried departures by master and dog on missions which often proved dangerous became practically routine at the Holman home.

One of the more important cases which developed after training graduation involved South London's notorious Ram Gang.
The specialty of these "teddy boys" (English terminology for
juvenile hoods or toughs) was to break into tobacconists' stores
and make off with cartons of cigarettes. They struck swiftly,
driving up to a store in a car during the night hours, smashing
the door open with a crowbar, looting it thoroughly and then
speeding away. They eluded police for weeks until they raided a
tobacconist's store in the Balham area. Inspector Elliot of the
Balham station became suspicious of their car. At 2:30 A.M., as
he approached it, he saw three men duck out of the store loaded
with cartons of cigarettes. The inspector, who was in a car,
slammed on the brakes and rushed from the vehicle. The
thieves were too quick for him and ran away in different directions before he could overtake any of them.

Elliot promptly put through a 999 call—the rush call for
police—and requested that Rex and Holman be sped to the
scene, even though other dogs and handlers were available at
that time.

The team was on the scene at 2:50 A.M. Holman put the dog
on his tracking line—a long leash designed to give the dog considerable freedom of movement and avoid the possibility of his
rushing off into darkness leaving his master ignorant of exactly
where he was heading. After sniffing around the thieves' automobile and inside of it, Rex was off on a scent, Holman and
other policemen following. Leading them through various
alleys and across a fence, he suddenly stopped and began barking before the door of an outside lavatory.

The door was locked and Holman smashed it open with a
powerful shoulder heave. A teddy boy was cowering against a
wall, holding his shoes in one hand, long hair tumbling over
his eyes. One look at Rex, fangs bared and snarling, prompted
a quavering cry: "Take that dog away, please take that dog
a-w-a-a-y!"

Holman told him the dog would do him no harm if he came away quietly. His hands trembled so badly that he could barely tighten the laces of his shoes when he was ordered to put them on. Looking at the trembling youth whose velvet-lapelled suit was a sorry sight by that time, Holman said, "If only the girls at the street corner could see you now." Then he turned him over to another policeman and hurried back to the car with Rex.

Here the dog sniffed around again and took off on another scent in a different direction. He guided Holman and other policemen to a house. The police entered and found and captured crook number two. Rex was led back to the car in an attempt to find the trail of a third man but by then the lapse of time and the comings and goings of the police had spoiled the scenting possibilities and his work was at an end that night. The third man was soon rounded up, however. His friends cracked under police questioning regarding his identity and hangouts and all three were clapped into prison for a year.

Another exciting case—impressively demonstrating a dog's usefulness in certain situations—occurred during a bitter cold spell at Christmas time in 1951. When Arthur and Betty went to bed on the night of December 20 they both expressed devout hopes that there would be no call to action during the night hours. It was not to be. At 4:30 A.M. a police car drew up at the front door, Rex barked and Holman knew that he must vacate his warm bed in a hurry. Donning his warmest apparel, including rubber boots, he hurried out with Rex and the car sped away through the night along ice-sheathed roads.

The driver told Holman that all he knew about the situation was that a safe had been burned open in one of the buildings of the big Dorman Long constructional engineering complex in Battersea. He had been ordered to pick up Arthur and Rex and proceed as fast as possible to Cringle Street, where the building in which the safe had been cracked was located.

Snow, which had stopped before midnight, was falling again

when the car skidded to a stop in Cringle Street at 4:55 A.M.
Between thirty and forty policemen were assembled in the vicinity, the area in which the Dorman Long main offices were
situated.

Every eye focused on Rex and Holman as they emerged from
the car, Rex straining at a shortened tracking leash, obviously
alert and excited and, being a seasoned copper, aware that
something was afoot.

At this time there still prevailed considerable doubts in many
police minds about the whole police dog operation. As Holman
strode through the falling snow toward an inspector in charge
he overheard some sarcastic remarks such as "What's the use of
calling in a blasted dog?" and "Blimey, what can a dog do in this
weather?" Holman kept his opinions to himself and queried the
inspector as to what was afoot.

"Three men were disturbed by the watchman at about 2:50
A.M. this morning," he replied. "They've burned a hole in the
safe with one of the firm's oxyacetylene burners. They ran from
the offices to the yard at the back and although we have been
searching since 3 A.M. we can't find a soul either in the building
or the big yard beyond. I think they've gone although we were
here fast enough. Do you think the dog can help us?"

"We'll soon find out, Inspector," Holman replied. "Better
get everyone out of the yard. I don't want Rex to attack a
policeman by mistake when he is searching."

The inspector agreed and all policemen were promptly ordered to vacate the yard. This was a huge area cluttered with all
types of machinery, including cranes, and construction supplies
of many types, offering untold opportunities for concealment.

Holman had good grounds for some trepidation over the entire situation. For two hours the area and some neighboring
terrain had been carefully gone over by numerous policemen.
The search had yielded absolutely nothing. Now a lone dog
would take over. If Rex failed, the tongues of critics would wag;

both Rex and other dogs on the force, despite fine records, would lose a lot of prestige. It was still snowing, the yard and its impedimenta ghostly white in the darkness. No question that the weather conditions were about as bad as could be in regard to dog sleuthing.

Rex's eyes glittered in the darkness, his magnificent muscles coiled for action. Holman gave the dog a pat and unleashed him.

"Good dog. Find him!"

The order was very familiar to the dog and he bounded off, a weaving blur in the snowflakes.

What followed would have been fit material for a film comedy short—barring the fact that some tough customers were the quarry.

Rex raced no more than thirty yards before he slithered to a halt and gave tongue. Holman rushed up and noticed that Rex was barking at the base of a medium-sized crane. Holman's flashlight beams on the lower part of the crane revealed nothing but shining upward they showed that the dog had scored a bull's-eye. Overhead a man, almost invisible in the darkness, his clothes dusted with snow, lay lengthwise on one of the arms of the crane.

A curt "Come on down, you" from Holman and the man half slithered to the ground. His teeth chattering, he stood submissively before the constable, muttering fearfully, "Keep that dog away from me."

"What the devil are you doing here?" Holman queried, his flashlight focused on the man's face and shoulders.

"I was looking for driftwood on the foreshore of the river," he replied, referring to a section of the Thames River nearby.

"There was no need for you to stay up there, that's no way to go after driftwood and besides the tide's been out for a long time. Come along," Holman said bitingly.

Grasping the man by one arm, Holman, with Rex growling

by his side, led the man to the group of police officers awaiting developments at the entrance to the yard.

"I believe this is one of the birds you were looking for," Holman said, inwardly amused at the thought that the man must have had a truly sweeping view of the previous police search.

"My word, that was quick work," the inspector in charge said as a murmur of astonishment came from the other onlookers.

"Thank Rex," Holman said. "Let's see if he can nail the other two now."

The team re-entered the yard but a sweeping search did not reveal any other fugitive. Rex did not give up, however, and picked up a scent which led him and his master over and around heaps of gear to the yard's far wall. They climbed across the wall, crossed Nine Elms Lane, scrambled over a fence and made for the river, Rex obviously on a good scent. Holman, numbed by the bitter cold in spite of warm clothing, stumbled and slithered after his dog, through various dumps pocked by bomb holes caused by wartime aerial blitzing, to the south bank of the Thames.

The trail led upriver and although they negotiated numerous other obstacles, including hillocks of evil-smelling waste, the scent suddenly became confused. Obviously other footsteps had blurred it badly.

Aware that Rex could do no more for the time, Holman led him back to the yard and reported to the inspector, somewhat depressed but still determined to try again.

"Did your men work upriver?" he asked the inspector.

"Yes, they did," was the reply.

"Oh, that's damned unfortunate, the dog has been following their scent," Holman asserted. "What about downriver?"

"We've already searched the whole area and we can't find them," the inspector said. "Anyway, your dog already has done excellent work—he caught one of them."

Like all good policemen, Holman had a stubborn streak in him, a determination to leave no possibility unexplored.

"Inspector, we have not finished yet," he said. "I'm going to search downriver with Rex."

Accompanied this time by other policemen, Holman then helped Rex across a wall and he and the others followed the dog into a littered yard on the other side. Before them loomed a building which the men later learned was a soap factory. Holman unleashed Rex and his "Find him!" sent Rex streaking away in the obscurity.

The yard was black and silent as the grave and the beam of my torch [flashlight] was like a solid, material thing as it followed the dog's progress. Rex reached a steel ladder and attempted to climb it, but the rungs were iced over and he kept slipping back. I called to one of the others:

"Can we get to the roof from inside the building?"

"Yes," came the reply. "But we've already searched up there."

I said nothing but, knowing that Rex must have followed a scent to the ladder, I climbed it myself. Paradoxically, the frozen steel seem to burn my hands and the last few yards to the top were indescribably painful. The factory was a large one, its roof made of glass, and as my eyes strained into the night I thought I could make out two figures crouched behind a low wall at the far side. I skidded down the ladder and entered the factory. Leaving two policemen on guard, Rex and I led others to the roof.

"Good dog. Find them!"—and within five seconds Rex was barking and growling at the wanted men who were, indeed, bent double behind the wall.

One of them half screamed, half sobbed, "Call the dog off! I'm afraid of dogs! I had one shock tonight when the safe blew back!"

At Nine Elms police station the three hoods were searched and charged. It was no happy chance that they had found the oxyacetylene gear: two of them had previously been employed by Dorman Long. All the money they had seized was recovered.

The three men were hustled immediately to Southwestern Magistrate's Court in Balham High Road for the formalities of arrest and charging. After the magistrate on duty, Mr. Clyde Wilson, had remanded the prisoners into custody he asked Holman to "bring that very useful and intelligent dog into court."

When Rex, who had been ordered to sit in a hall just outside the courtroom, was brought before the magistrate he received an approving pat from the official. Dead tired, longing for a shot of brandy and some hot tea, Holman briefly answered some questions from the magistrate regarding Rex and then headed for home with his dog in a police car. The magistrate never forgot Rex and would invariably ask Holman when they met on later occasions, "How is that excellent dog Rex these days?"

After a second appearance at South London the men were committed for trial at the Old Bailey and Rex made history as the first canine "witness" ever to appear at the Central Criminal Court. Rex went along in case the prisoners alleged that he had bitten or savaged them. In this case I would have demonstrated to the jury that he would turn nasty only when ordered to or in self-defence. However, the men pleaded guilty and I was not called upon either to give evidence or actually bring Rex, who was in the building, before the judge. Two of the men received sentences of three years and the other went to prison for 18 months.

The performance of Rex won plaudits from high police officials and the whole operation was the subject of dramatic newspaper accounts, embellished with photographs of the dog and his master. Before Christmas day stacks of fan mail arrived at the Holman residence. There were requests for snapshots and paw-mark "autographs" and offers of money if Holman would mate Rex with this or that privately owned female Alsatian. One little girl asked for a lock of Rex's hair, which was sent to her. Many persons also sent money orders and the funds from these were pigeonholed for Rex's weekly marrowbone. This marrowbone was a special treat in his daily meal, which he always received at night around 10 P.M.

Holman has an amusing photograph of his daughter Vivienne scanning some fan mail, seated at a table in their home. Rex is sitting on the table looking at opened envelopes and their contents. He is quite serious about the whole thing and seems in a detached way to understand what it is all about.

Rex was something of an oddity as far as eating was concerned. Sometimes he would go for 48 hours without solid food and there was nothing Holman could do about it. This occurred even though he was in perfect health. Fortunately, he was consistent in drinking a pint of milk every day. He was allowed only one bone a week. His jaws and teeth, Holman decided, were strong enough without exercising them on bones. His master did not want him to swallow bone splinters, which can prove harmful to a dog's stomach. Arthur would crack open the bone with a cold chisel and let Rex get at the marrow, which he did, usually ignoring the rest. His daily meat portion usually consisted of liver, for which he had a great liking.

Police veterinary advice or aid was always available but the main care of the dog was undertaken by Holman himself or by members of his family. During summer months Rex was bathed every six weeks with soap and tepid water. He was never bathed between October and March. This was a precaution against a night call in which Rex might be obliged to face winter weather before he was completely dry, increasing the possibility of his catching a bad chill or cold.

Whenever Rex had been out in rain or snow, as was the case in the gun attack and at Dorman Long's, Holman dried him carefully and thoroughly with a chamois leather, paying particular attention to his chest and loins, the weak spots for chills. During his daily grooming Holman would first brush him against the coat to clear the undercoat of dust and grit, then comb and brush him and polish his coat with a chamois cloth. Eyes, ears and feet were cleaned daily. Off duty, Rex was exercised every three hours and when on rather infrequent occasions he indicated by a bark or yowl that he wanted to go outside, Holman immediately took him for a stroll. "It is as dangerous for an animal to have to 'hold itself back' as it is for a child," was one of Holman's sage opinions regarding dog care in general.

Like Dox and most other dogs, Rex was a sucker for children and never lost his temper with any one of them. One of his favorites was a two-year-old nephew of Arthur's, named Andrew, who was a weekend guest of the Holmans on many occasions during that year of his life. Andrew loved to crawl into Rex's kennel, evidently considering it a delightfully mysterious "manor" tailored to size. When Andrew toddled toward the kennel, Rex would politely vacate it if he was inside at the time and let Andrew enter it. If Andrew was inside when the dog returned from a patrol he would invariably sit or lie down outside the kennel and wait for Andrew to come out at his leisure.

Rex and another police dog of the Metropolitan force performed smoothly together in a brisk night hunt in May, 1952. The other dog was a female, a beautiful light-gray Alsatian named Jenny three months younger than Rex. She belonged to Constable "Jock" MacCallum, a good friend of Holman's operating in the neighboring R Division.

Generally, policemen preferred to leave their dogs with a friend in the canine division when they went on holiday. When MacCallum left for a holiday that May, Holman agreed to take care of his dog at his home. This provoked no trouble since Rex knew Jock and his dog. Jenny was placed in Rex's kennel and Rex was put indoors. On the first night everything was quiet until 2:30 A.M. the following morning when both dogs suddenly began barking in deafening unison. A patrol car had pulled up at the gate. Another call to action.

As Holman hurriedly struggled into his clothes his wife asked, "What in heaven's name are we going to do with Jenny? I'm afraid she'll continue barking now that she is excited. She'll have all the neighborhood awake."

"Don't worry, Betty, I'll take her with us; they say two heads are better than one, you know," Holman replied.

The car sped Holman and the two dogs to Merton Abbey, where an inspector named Wood was waiting after putting in a rush call for Rex. He informed Arthur that a man dressed in a sports jacket and dungarees had broken into the factory of Messrs. Lamden and Company. A watchman had spotted him and had tried to detain him but the intruder escaped over a fence and dashed toward Merton Abbey Goods and Coal Yard.

Holman wasted no time. Removing the leashes from the two dogs, he said, "Find him!" to Rex and, "Seek!" to Jenny, the word MacCallum had trained her to heed. With hand gestures Holman made the dogs streak off in different directions. Within a few minutes he heard Rex bark and shortly thereafter Jenny's barks mingled with those of Rex, coming from the same direction, the female apparently having joined the other dog to help him in whatever was afoot.

Holman scrambled over coal heaps and railway tracks to the spot from which the barks were coming and found that the two dogs had a man nailed under a truck. The man was lying flat on his stomach, crying for help although he had not been hurt. As soon as Holman had assured him the dogs would be kept off him, he crawled out, one of the most scared men the constable had ever seen. The sight of one Alsatian in attack pattern is bad enough but two snarling and barking simultaneously is sufficient to shatter the toughest nerves, Holman realized.

The constable and the two dogs made a further search of the area in quest for accomplices but this yielded nothing. The man, who had not been able to steal anything because of the alert watchman, insisted that he had operated alone. He was arrested and eventually sentenced to 18 months' imprisonment. To Holman and other policemen the case was of special interest since it proved that two dogs of different sex could work well together.

In November, 1952, the papers were full of stories about the raids on various stores, including jewelry shops, by what was nicknamed "The Phantom Car Gang." In every instance the gang, driving a fast Jaguar, escaped. By November 27, however, the police had sufficient leads and decided to close in on the gang. Holman, Rex and Detective-Sergeants Walters and Bridges and Constable Donald Cameron were instructed to lay a trap for the criminals. They were assigned to watch a garage at Maitland Court, which is a block of flats in Addison Road, Notting Hill. The police knew that the car, which had been stolen, was housed in this garage by the robbers. The police in this instance did not want merely to arrest the men as car thieves but to catch them red-handed as store looters, which would entail a more severe sentence.

This would necessitate a secret vigil in which the garage could be kept under observation. The watch began the night of November 27, a bitterly cold one, with occasional rain squalls. Rex and Holman took positions on the top floor of a roofless, bombed house which had never been repaired. From their vantage point, they could clearly see the garage and nearby buildings. The other policemen took up positions at the base of the ruined building, also closely watching the area. The night hours dragged along with the men and the dog patiently enduring considerable physical discomfort, chilled by freezing rainfalls. Also real danger was present—the men of the gang were of violent stamp and were known at one time to have stated that they would not hesitate to run down a policeman with their car or knock him out of action with weapons if the occasion arose.

The first night's watch drew a blank. A few cars passed but no Jaguar entered or left the garage. At dawn the men and Rex, who had remained quiet but alert by the side of his master throughout the tedious hours, returned either to their stations or their homes. It was agreed to resume the vigil at 6 P.M. November 28, observing the greatest secrecy possible.

Again the night was cold, rainfalls transformed into sheets of hail. Finally, at 8:25 P.M., the watchers, occupying the same positions as the previous night, were rewarded. The doors of the garage were opened from the inside and a Jaguar slid out. Bidding Rex to stay where he was, Holman hurried downstairs to confer with his colleagues. It was unanimously decided to mark time and await the car's return since the four men in it were in all probability bent on a raid and would return with the loot that night.

When the car had vanished down the road Holman returned to his rooftop observation post and resumed his watch with Rex. The police had guessed rightly. At 10:30 the same Jaguar and its riders appeared in the street and drove back into the garage. Once inside, the doors were closed again by one of the occupants.

The time to strike had come. Holman, who was wearing civilian clothing as were his colleagues in this operation, knew what to do. He hurried into the street with Rex and began strolling at a leisurely pace down Addison Road past the Maitland Court buildings, heading for the garage. To all intents and purposes just another civilian giving his dog an airing. He had advanced a short distance when he saw two men moving in shadow areas near the garage.

"Then I heard the running feet of the C.I.D. men behind me, Walters, Bridges and Cameron," Holman wrote. "The two crooks hesitated only for a moment. One shouted 'This way!' and they both tore across the road and down a side alley."

Holman spun around retaining Rex as Walters, Bridges and

Cameron rushed by shouting to the fugitives to halt.* Walters and Bridges soon caught up with one of the fleeing men and subdued him in a brief but violent struggle. The second man, chased by Cameron, however, was very fleet and began to outstrip the constable.

"Stop him!" Holman snapped and Rex bolted. There was no necessity for Holman to tell him what his quarry was—the dog's meticulous training plus experience in many similar episodes would guide him in this matter. Rex ignored the two detective-sergeants still wrestling with their prisoner, swept past the pounding Cameron, and went like an arrow for the fleeing crook.

Holman sprinted after his dog, confident that everything would be over in a few minutes. The running fugitive, with hardly a pause in his stride, clambered over a six-foot gate and vanished from Holman's view. Close on his trail, Rex immediately leaped up on one of the walls flanking the gate and also disappeared from view on the other side, where some houses were located.

In a few seconds Holman scrambled over the gate, guided by snarls from Rex and a string of foul language. About 40 yards from the wall Rex had the man cornered against a trash can, his fangs firmly gripping one of the fugitive's jacket lapels.

Rex loosed his hold on command, and Holman, seizing one of the man's arms and warning him that resistance was useless, marched him back to the gate, Rex circling the pair. Walters then rushed up and climbed over to help Holman control the prisoner. Ordered to scramble over the gate, the man suddenly made a desperate effort to run free and a scuffle ensued between him and the two policemen. In forcing him over the gate, Walters fell, cracking a bone in his wrist.

---

* London's police have refrained from carrying revolvers up to the time of this writing. This ruling may have been changed by the time this book is published as a result of the killing of a number of policemen in 1966.

Obeying a stern order from Holman, Rex refrained from joining in the tussle and then followed the trio via one of the walls. Cameron joined the group but he also had had an accident. His right arm hung limp, badly injured when he had tripped over an obstacle and fallen hard on stone paving.

Only four minutes had elapsed since the pursuit began. The action was not over, however, especially for Rex. As the men and the dog headed for the vicinity of the garage where Bridges was holding the other man prisoner, two other men materialized from the shadows and sprinted down Addison Road.

Holman shouted, "Stop them!" and Rex was on their track. He checked the first man by leaping on his back and tumbling him to the ground.

Petrified by vicious snaps from Rex inches from his face, the man lay still and began to cry. Rex plunged after the second crook and seized his wrist in his teeth. Soon the four prisoners were lined up against a wall, under control but glowering and still dangerous.

Holman told his colleagues he would go to a nearby house and try to phone for police transport. Before leaving he enjoined Rex, "Guard them!"—a vital command at this juncture since for a brief while the desperadoes would outnumber the policemen, two of whom were not in top shape due to arm injuries.

A minor but irritating complication now arose. He knocked at the door of a nearby house, hoping the occupants had a phone. The door was opened by a boy of about eight, behind him his baby sister of about five. They obviously were alone in the house and terrified by the presence of a grimy man in rumpled clothes at the door. Holman tried to pacify them and convince them he was a policeman. They were too scared to understand and Arthur gently told them to go back to bed and forget about the whole thing.

Holman returned to his colleagues and the prisoners and

Walters went off to try to halt a passing car. As he hurried away one of the prisoners leaped aside, sprinted across a yard, clambered over a wall and disappeared in some gardens of Maitland Court beyond it. Another "Stop him!" and Rex again was in action. He hurtled over the wall and when Holman caught up with him he was standing over the sprawled body of the prisoner, teeth bared, and growling.

This concluded the fracas at Maitland Court. Walters contacted a passing motorist who got on a phone and dialed 999. In some 15 minutes the police had the men safely inside the Notting Hill Gate police station.

The ambush was a complete success—the men had been caught red-handed. In the back of the Jaguar police found a silver rose-bowl and two silver cups worth about £500 (about $1,400), stolen that very night in a raid on a hairdressing exhibition in Albermarle Street.

When the men were formally charged, the leader of the gang, a somewhat "likable villain" according to Holman, told him: "No copper could catch me. It took a dog to do that. And if you're going to use dogs regularly I'm going straight."

The leader was sentenced to four years' imprisonment and his accomplices to four years, two years, and eighteen months, respectively.

As in the case of so many criminals, the promise to go straight was a hollow one. Released from prison in 1955 before completing his full sentence, the leader went on an armed robbery spree. He was captured in a gun duel by Detective-Sergeant Albert Eric Chambers and Police-Constable Cameron, the same policeman who had suffered an arm injury in the Maitland Court episode. The sentence for this was much stiffer—ten years.

For Holman the Maitland Court ambush was particularly gratifying. It was the first time that the Ghost Squad of Scotland Yard—one of the crack units—had asked him and his dog to cooperate in an important operation. Everyone was markedly impressed and there were fresh plaudits from higher-ups at the Yard and from the press for Rex.

Rex continued to perform well in many missions until 1956 when a relentless foe of man and beast brought him down: cancer.

In May Rex showed signs of illness, the main difficulty coughing and some difficulty in breathing. In spite of the best possible care from the Holmans and the services of top veterinarians, his condition worsened steadily. Early in October came the verdict which Holman feared—cancer of the throat. The veterinary who informed Holman of the diagnosis said it would be futile to operate. The best thing that could be done would be to put Rex to sleep. Holman agreed, deep sorrow in his heart. On October 7 he drove his beloved dog to the police training center at Keston. There he turned the dog over to a sergeant on duty and said:

"It's finished with our Rex III. Would you please take him to the vets? He has to be put to sleep. I just can't do it myself."

The sergeant nodded gravely and bestowed a compassionate glance on the ailing dog. Holman, with a gulp in his throat, patted Rex's head and stroked one of his ears.

"I said, 'Good dog,'" Holman wrote. "He looked up at me questioningly, as he always did when I moved from his side. 'Good dog,' I repeated. 'Stay.'"

Almost unable to move, Rex wagged his tail feebly and lay still on the ground, his head between his paws. As Holman stood in a nearby door ready to leave the room he exchanged a last glance with his dog, tears filling the veteran policeman's eyes.

"He is buried in the woods at Keston," Holman wrote. "I do not know where nor do I want to know."

Grief in the Holman household was profound. Letters of condolence came in from many parts of Britain. Eventually

Holman obtained and trained a new dog, an Alsatian named Boss. Both dog and man gave valuable service to the police before Holman retired a few years ago.

"As regards Rex, ours was no ordinary 'master and pet' relationship," he wrote at the end of his book. "Police Dog Rex III was an essential part of my life and being, and still dominates my thoughts and memories. When he died something vital went from me, for in Rex I really did 'give my heart to a dog to tear.' "

In any account of the police dog operations in England after World War II the accomplishments of Ben, the black Labrador, will always have an honored place alongside those of Rex. Both were champion dogs. Whether one was really greater than the other is largely a matter of personal viewpoint. The arrests credited to Ben were as numerous as those of Rex.

Ben was enrolled in 1947 and won early note in tackling sneak thieves in Hyde Park, particular pests to lovers strolling in this large and verdant area of the metropolis.

After three months of training the Labrador retriever and his handler, Shelton, were on a regular patrol in the park, a reassuring factor to all except the lawless. Each night they patrolled the pathways, ignoring lovers blissfully attentive to each other and strolling pairs or groups; always on the lookout for sneak thieves whose modus operandi was to slip off their shoes, pad quietly up to some preoccupied couple and snatch a purse.

Ben soon showed a remarkable ability to spot a guilty person. Frequently as the team canvassed the park Ben would come to a sudden halt and growl deeply, a warning that trouble was afoot. Shelton learned to respect Ben's judgment.

"Ben can sense the physical reaction of the culprit," he explained. "If a man is guilty he feels fear at the sight of policeman and dog. Ben can smell this fear."

At Shelton's command, Ben would be off into the bushes.

When the constable caught up in the chase he would usually find a thief, quaking in his socks. Having delivered his prisoner, the dog would then sniff around and fetch any handbag that had been cast away. Then he would roam about and find any articles which might have been thrown out of the purse in the general vicinity and retrieve these.

The dog also became the unrelenting enemy of the London "spivs" dealing in black-market cigarettes and nylons. Catching a spiv in the act of trading was one thing for the police; spotting him on the prowl was quite another problem.

The spivs soon developed an abiding fear of Ben's fine nose and uncanny perspicacity.

"Ben could spot a spiv at 50 paces," Shelton said. "His growl became a signal to me to stop a man for questioning. Sometimes I wondered whether Ben didn't know precisely whether it was hosiery or tobacco the chap was concealing."

The dog's radarlike ability to sense guilt in persons became legendary at Scotland Yard. Once he went along merely for the ride when Shelton drove into the London suburbs to question a witness about a series of crimes committed in the vicinity. The witness proved difficult and taciturn. Finally the dog's constable-handler suggested that it might be a good idea if the man came along to the police station for a talk with the sergeant.

"When the man got into our car my dog expressed uneasiness, flicking his eyes at the man and growling from the tail up," Shelton recalled. "He was restless during the station interview, and when the chap departed Ben let out indignant howls. I didn't like the man, neither did the sergeant, but we had not a thing against him that would hold up."

Weeks later, the fractious witness broke down when he was again hauled in for questioning. He confessed that he was the perpetrator of a whole series of crimes which had puzzled the police and was sentenced to ten years' imprisonment.

Ben's special "judo" maneuver—thrusting his head between a

fugitive's legs and thus toppling him—was developed on his own initiative and was not the result of any special training. He never quite abandoned this tumbling technique but a series of painful kicks to the nose caused him to use it more circumspectly as the years passed.

"Ben never 'savaged' a captive although there were times when his ingrained decency in this regard was sorely tried," Shelton said. "One criminal kicked Ben viciously when overtaken and fled again. This time when Ben outran him he reverted to his old trick with the head. When I arrived the chap was sprawled on the ground and Ben's teeth were playing a tattoo up and down his shinbone. But he really never harmed the man, as well he might have."

One of Ben's most spectacular exploits occurred in 1951 in a police hunt for a dangerous young criminal named Frederick Poole. Poole had escaped from jail and was believed to be hiding somewhere in Middlesex. Warned that he might be armed, police patrolled the area constantly while householders lived in terror.

Then, on a Saturday night, the alarm sounded in Sunbury, Middlesex, a suburb of London comparable to the suburb of Bronxville near New York City. Poole had broken into a house and had stolen food and a suit of clothes. In doing so he had dropped a handkerchief bearing a prison marking.

Police threw out a cordon; three police dogs were rushed to the scene (Rex III was not involved in this operation although he was available at this time). For hours the teams combed Sunbury but Poole eluded them. Late on Sunday the call went out for Shelton and Ben.

They arrived just before dawn on Monday. Ben sniffed the handkerchief and was off. He led Shelton through cluttered backyards, over hedges, across fields, through clusters of trees. Finally the handler heard the dog, who was off leash, bark and saw a figure run from behind a clump of bushes. A few minutes later he saw the figure fall with Ben on top of him. The action was so swift that Shelton never knew whether the man had been toppled by the familiar head thrust or by another method. When Shelton and another policeman came up, the dog was on top of the man, snarling in his face. It was Poole—captured without a shot being fired. A long prison term followed for Poole.

The usefulness of dogs in police work was underscored in a statement made by Chief Inspector S. E. Peck of Scotland Yard when Ben had been credited with his 100th arrest.

"This dog," he said, "has set a better record than most police constables achieve in their entire service."

Rex and Holman

> When the Man waked up he said, "What is Wild
> Dog doing here?" And the Woman said. "His name
> is not Wild Dog any more, but the First Friend,
> because he will be our friend for always and
> always and always."
>
> —RUDYARD KIPLING, *Just So Stories*

8

Brandy 4, Nero, Christel and Some Others

THE number of successful results achieved by the Dog Section has risen progressively each year and perhaps the most pleasing feature of these increased achievements is to be found in the fact that more and more incidents are being brought to a successful conclusion through work of the dog itself; this is particularly true in the field of tracking and in the searching of buildings and open spaces. . . . In addition to patrolling, searching, chasing, controlling small groups of people, dogs can be used for recovering stolen property which has been abandoned and for finding missing persons. Over the years, the use to which properly trained and handled dogs can be put are becoming more and more apparent and with further experience and continued experiments in new methods of deployment, their scope will be increasingly widened.

These statements augur well for escalation of police dog operations—at least in England—for they are contained in informative textual material provided this author by the Metropolitan Police Office, New Scotland Yard, London, S.W. 1, and received in January, 1966.

In the last ten years the dog division has expanded markedly and today is the most important in the world. In 1965 the number of dogs enrolled ranged from 206 to 210, a startling increase over the relatively small number of dogs used ten to twelve years ago.

The documents provide interesting statistics regarding dog and handler operations in 1965. The tabulation, listing accomplishments of the division from January through September in Districts 1, 2, 3, and 4 of the Metropolitan Police, is as follows:

Arrests made by dogs	261
Arrests with dogs' assistance	651
Arrests in which dogs did not assist but were present	1663
Missing persons found	50
Items of property found	107

The numerous cases where dogs were present but did not assist constitute no reflection on the canines. Presumably these were occurrences in which a dog or dogs were hurried to the scene but became inoperative because of various developments, such as surrender of a fugitive, lack of any scent trail or a last-minute twist to the entire case making canine sleuthing useless. It is quite probable that the mere knowledge that a police dog or dogs were around ready for action on many occasions was a nagging psychological worry to criminals if lawlessness was involved in the operation. As has been shown in previous accounts, it is no easy matter to flee from a house or down a street if trained dogs and handlers are around. A quick "Stop him!" can in split seconds transform such a dog from onlooker into a frightening hunter.

There is human drama and excitement behind the laconic verbiage listing of some of the incidents which occurred in the nine-month period. They appear as follows in Scotland Yard records:

SEARCH—MISSING PERSON FOUND

At 12:35 A.M. on January 17, "Simon 2" and his handler were called to No. 123 Seaford Road, Ealing, W. 13, where the daughter of the house had informed Police that her mother, aged 94, was missing. It appeared that the daughter had left her mother in the house at 9 P.M. to visit a neighbor and on her return at 10:45 P.M. was unable to find her, despite inquiries of the neighbors and the local police and a search of the house, garden and nearby areas. "Simon" was put to search the area at the rear of the house and within three minutes gave tongue. The handler discovered the dog standing by this elderly lady who was lying on an overgrown path about 100 yards from the house. She was in a semi-conscious condition, her clothing soaked with rain and she had minor abrasions. There appears to be no doubt that this successful search saved the life of this very elderly lady.

SEARCH—1 ARREST

At 8 P.M. on January 25 "Christel" and her handler were called to assist the crew of area car W5 who were searching the Woodcote Hotel, Chalk Lane, Epsom. Three men had been arrested for stealing lead from the roof of this partly derelict property and a fourth man was thought to have escaped. The handler put "Christel" to search the house, beginning in the cellars and working up through the building: the car crew assisted also. Upon reaching the attics, "Christel" became very alert and began jumping up at the walls. In the light of their torches, the officers could see several small holes in the ceiling and at this time the dog began to give tongue. The officers were able to get through a fan-light on to the roof and also to get "Christel" through with them. A small hole was found in the slates and the dog was put in to search the large area beneath, although the hole appeared too small for a man to pass through. Within a few minutes "Christel" gave tongue and a man's voice asked for the dog to be called off. The suspect, a very small person, then came out and was arrested.

SEARCH—1 ARREST

At 6:30 P.M. on February 4 "Lucky 4" with "Nero" and their respective handlers were patrolling in the R/T Dog Van when a call was received to assist police at Great Suffolk Street, S.E. 1, where a robbery had taken place. The watchman on the premises had been tied up and the safe keys taken by three men. Whilst on the premises, these men had been disturbed by a lorry driver and one had run into the street and two had disappeared. Police had searched the building and recovered the safe keys, and a man's cap, but there was no trace of the suspects. "Lucky 4" was put to search the interior of the premises and "Nero" was taken by his handler to search the outside yards. After about 45 minutes "Lucky" led his handler into the basement and out into a "well" situated between the two buildings. The dog then mounted a fire escape and at the top became very alert and gave tongue. The handler, by the light of his torch, noticed a drain pipe running at an angle to the roof and there appeared to be fresh "scuff" marks leading to the roof. The handler then passed this information on to the other police officers, who obtained a ladder and climbed onto the roof. "Lucky" and his handler remained on the fire escape, keeping watch. Two suspects were found on the roof and one attempted to come down the fire escape but on seeing "Lucky" below submitted to arrest.

TRACK—2 ARRESTS

At 11:30 P.M. on March 11 "Arnold" and his handler were patrolling in a police car in London Road, Croydon, and stopped to assist two police officers who were questioning two youths. The youths were in a dirty condition, but both refused to say where they had been. "Arnold" was put to track from the youths and led his handler along London Road, into Mead Place, and from there to Parsons Mead, a distance of about 280 yards. "Arnold" then led his handler to the rear of a machine factory and to a broken window. On the ground outside the window, a large quantity of metal fittings were found which had been stolen from the factory and stacked in readiness to take away. The two youths then admitted to breaking into the premises.

CHASE & TRACK—1 ARREST

At 11:50 A.M. on March 5 "Giles" and his handler, who was off duty, saw three men fighting on the footway in Downhills Park Road, N. 15. Two of the men were aids to the C.I.D. and the third was being arrested for housebreaking. The officers indicated another man who was running away down the middle of the road. The handler sent "Giles" to stop this man and the dog effected this quickly, taking the suspect on the right sleeve. The man swung the dog against a barrier for pedestrians, knocking him off, but "Giles" again held his prisoner by the sleeve, and for the second time was swung against the barrier and knocked off. A third time "Giles" seized the suspect by the sleeve and this time was swung hard against a metal post. "Giles" fell winded to the pavement. By the time the handler was able to get his dog on his feet, the suspect had disappeared, but "Giles" was put to track. The dog tracked through the thick slush, through a park and across other areas, through the front door of a house and out through the back door into the garden, where the suspect was found hiding in a coal bunker.

SEARCH—PROPERTY RECOVERED

At 11:30 P.M. on April 10 "Brandy 4" and his handler were patrolling in Granville Road, S.W. 18. The officer found a large torch in the garden of No. 94 which was in the vicinity of a recent housebreaking. "Brandy" was put to search the gardens adjacent to No. 94 and the dog returned shortly with a small silver dish. The dog continued searching and in the garden of No. 86 he found a larger silver dish. "Brandy" proceeded through the gardens and at

No. 80 found a glove and a little later three more gloves. The dog then jumped over a wall and tried to reach the center of a dense bush and gave tongue. Upon investigation by the handler, a full bottle of whisky was found. When these items of property were shown to three suspects already in custody, they admitted ownership of the torch and gloves and the other items as part of the property stolen from No. 94 Granville Road.

SEARCH—MISSING PERSONS FOUND

At 11 P.M. on June 10 "Duke 19" and his handler were called from home to assist in a search for two children missing from their home since 1:30 P.M. The handler took "Duke" to search the eastern end of Clapham Common and the adjoining area. The dog could not be set free because of the number of people in the vicinity. At 12:05 A.M. the handler entered the grounds of Trinity Close to search the area and the lock-up garages at the rear. As the officer and his dog were passing a shrubbery, the dog gave tongue and indicated there was something in the bushes. Upon investigation the handler found the two missing girls, aged 8 and 10 years, asleep.

TRACK—DISCOVERY OF LOCATION OF "BREAKING"

At 11:30 P.M. on July 8 "Kim 50" and his handler were called to assist the crew of police car Q-11 who had arrested three men in possession of stolen property believed to be the proceeds of safe breaking. "Kim" was put to track from a passageway from where the prisoners had emerged and led his handler for a distance of about 800 yards to factory premises, where it was found that a breaking had occurred. A good example of back-tracking by "Kim 50."

SEARCH—4 ARRESTS—RECOVERY OF WEAPON

At 2:45 A.M. on July 18, "Nimrod" and "Angela," together with their handlers were called to Cherbury Street, N. 1, where a man had been fatally stabbed. As a result of inquiries four men were detained by the handlers. "Nimrod" and "Angela" were then put to search in the vicinity for the weapon used in the murder. At 3.30 A.M. "Nimrod" found a claw hammer, which was removed by a C.I.D. officer. "Tiger" and his handler then joined in the search for a knife, believed to be in a nearby block of flats. The grounds, balconies, stairs and rubbish bins were searched thoroughly until 8 A.M. but no trace of the knife was found. Later a fifth man was arrested and charged with murder.

CHASE—8 ARRESTS

At 11:45 P.M. on July 24 "Alfred" and his handler were patrolling when they encountered two gangs of men fighting. Upon the approach of the officers the gang dispersed and three men and one girl ran away. They ignored the handler's call to stop and "Alfred" was released to chase. As the dog approached the four persons stopped whilst the dog circled around them. They were arrested. "Alfred" with the handler then approached the remaining four men who also ignored the order to stand still and ran off. The dog was again released and repeated his earlier action of performing a "Stand Off" when the group stopped running. With the assistance of "Alfred" all eight persons were detained.

TRACK—1 ARREST

At 12:15 A.M. on September 13, "Rikki II" and his handler were called to the British Legion Club, Chelsfield, where a suspect had been arrested within the clubhouse and it was suspected that he may have had an accomplice or a vehicle. "Rikki" was put to track and found a scent leading his handler for about 300 yards over grass to a car which was parked on Court Road, Orpington. A second man was waiting in the car and was subsequently arrested.

The above accounts show clearly that trained dogs and competent handlers can cope very well with a wide variety of cases. As in other countries, funny situations do crop up in the serious business of law enforcement. No doubt the police got some laughs when Brandy 4 found the bottle of whisky and from another incident which had a rather comical climax during the "wee hours" of February 21, 1965.

At 12:40 A.M. Prince 89 and his handler were called to the premises of a wholesale drugstore in Old Kent Road, S.E. 1, where the automatic alarm had been blasting away. The handler took Prince to the rear of the premises, where someone had broken in. The dog found a scent and led his handler through several nearby gardens, finally stopping at an unused chicken run and gave tongue.

A suspect was found hiding in the chicken run, a very frightened man who quavered, "Keep that dog off me." He was promptly searched by the policemen. His loot: several bottles of liquid shampoo taken from the drugstore!

In the statement earlier in this chapter, the London police cited the fact that dogs can be used to control "small groups of persons." This could mean in some instances a number of lawbreakers. It does not signify that the use of dogs is advisable where larger crowds are involved. The attitude of Scotland Yard was made very clear in a letter received by this author from its Information Officer, dated January 5, 1966. It said:

"Although dogs are used by almost every Police Force in Great Britain, they are not trained, or used, for riot or crowd control."

"It is not advisable to use dogs where large groups of people are concerned as they become confused, especially if surrounded, and if trodden on accidentally or their handlers are jostled or assaulted, they tend to bite indiscriminately," the Metropolitan Police of London have decided.*

Specific orders have been issued to handlers not to use their canines to control crowds at political gatherings or sports events or if labor disputes are involved.

London police use both female and male dogs but this apparently is not a source of trouble when the bitches are in heat.

"With modern veterinary products no difficulties are experienced during the time the bitches are in 'season' and they usually remain on duty," Scotland Yard informed me.

The favorite tracking dog of Richardson and others in the "old days" are out in England as far as police work is concerned.

---

* Larger-type dogs have terrific mauling power in their jaws. It has been estimated that a well-developed German shepherd, biting hard, can exert from 500 to 600 pounds of pressure per square inch with its jaws.

"Bloodhounds are no longer used in Great Britain," the Public Information officer of the Yard informed me. "The German Shepherd Dog (Alsatian) is the most popular breed for police work and these are employed in large numbers. To a lesser degree, Labrador Retrievers and Dobermans are also used. As a point of interest, police officers and dogs from Washington, D.C. and St. Louis (Mo.) Police forces were trained at the Metropolitan Police Dog Training Establishment."

The organization of the dog division and its development, dog training techniques and other important aspects of the whole undertaking are discussed in detail in a special brochure compiled by the Yard. It reads as follows under the title *Metropolitan Police Dogs*:

INTRODUCTION

From time immemorial, dogs have been used by man for such varying purposes as sport and rescue work, for security, as beasts of burden, as war dogs, and, much more recently, as aids to the blind and to the police. It is known that as long ago as the 15th century, the parish constables patrolled with dogs which were probably used more for companionship than for police work, although it is certainly true that the constables of those times were more in need of protection than their colleagues of today.

The Metropolitan Police District which extends over an area of some 790 square miles, varies in character from open country on the outskirts to the crowded closely built-up streets of Central London. [London has a population of about 8,000,000. Ed.] It includes large housing estates, commercial areas, warehouses, docks, public gardens and parks, and the use of dogs as an aid to police has been progressively developed to cater for the many different problems which can arise in such different types of terrain.

Between the two world wars, Chief Officers of Police experimented with the use of the Bloodhound, Labrador, Boxer, Doberman, Rottweiler and German Shepherd dog: whereas it was first thought necessary to have different types of dogs and different types of training to produce dogs for the tasks of tracking, guard or patrol work, it has now been proved that a suitable dog can be successfully trained as an all-rounder. There may be scope for some specialist trained dogs, i.e. detecting hidden dangerous drugs but considerations of economy normally rule this out.* For City work the German Shepherd dog has proved to be the most adaptable and reliable.

It was not until 1946 when six trained Labradors were taken into service, that the first real attempt was made in the Metropolis to use the obvious qualities of a dog to provide expert aid to the policeman but they were employed in the outer areas as patrol dogs and were little more than companions to their handlers.

When Police dogs were first brought to Central London in 1948 they achieved spectacular success in Hyde Park, where the prevalent crime of handbag stealing was practically eliminated. Good work of this kind and a number of arrests on Divisional patrol as a result of tracking, searching for and pursuing criminals, encouraged the use of dogs on general purpose work throughout the whole of the Metropolitan Police District.

TYPES OF DOGS

It has often been said that a dog is only as good as its handler allows it to be, and for Police purposes it is essential not only to have a perfectly trained dog, but its handler must also be a capable Policeman. Dog and handler work as a team and a strong bond of sympathy must be forged between them.

The working standard achieved by Police dogs depends almost entirely upon the type of dog and the skill with which it is trained and handled. Every effort is being made in training to widen the field of knowledge relating to the breeding, rearing and training of dogs. Knowledge of dog behavior does not come easily and the field is so complex that there is still much to learn. It must be continuously impressed upon the handler that his dog is not a machine but

---

* Police dogs have been used in London to detect narcotics on persons or in buildings and also in the streets. Holman was ordered to give Rex III special training in dope detection in 1954 and in final tests Rex performed impressively before police officials. Holman implied in his book that his dog did operate in this field but gives no details. Logically, police maintain secrecy regarding such narcotics investigations.

a living animal which dislikes hunger, fear, pain and cold as much as humans do and, by the same token, appreciates the qualities of gentleness, kindness and decisiveness. Without this understanding a handler can ruin a promising dog. Like human beings, no two dogs are exactly alike and it is possible that more attention should be given to the study of dog behavior when seeking to improve training techniques of the future.

In commenting on the fact that the Alsatian has been proven to be the best all-rounder, the document continues:

Provided it comes from sound stock and has been properly treated in puppyhood the Alsatian will have intelligence, boldness and the keenness of the senses so necessary for training; its coat and conformation will allow it to stand up to rigorous tours of duty in all weather conditions; it will have a firm steady temperament and be amenable to discipline. Psychologically the Alsatian's appearance has a high deterrent value which seems to make him feared by wrong-doers.

The main problem of recent years had been to find a sufficiency of suitable dogs to meet the growing demands and the potentialities of other breeds for Police work have been considered, bearing in mind the criterion that the right dog must be suitable for Police purposes—a good temperament, a sound conformation and the possession of the natural qualities of the true working dog, which are much more important than appearance. To obtain this type of animal, selective breeding from proved working stock is essential once a good strain has been established. . . .

To help in achieving this object, seven bitches and three male dogs were purchased in 1960 in Germany. They were thoroughly examined medically and by X-ray and their blood lines carefully checked. Since then, by selective breeding, a number of dogs of fine physique and firm temperament have been bred. Many dogs will still be required from the home market, however, but preference will always be shown for those which have grown beyond puppyhood and which can be tested for the qualities required of them. Puppies must have had a full life in natural surroundings—urban and rural. The dog which is conditioned only to the kennel and the show ring will generally fall short of police requirements. If the right dogs can be found a realistic price will be paid for them.

SPECIAL QUALITIES OF DOGS

Perhaps the most important quality in a dog is its sense of smell.* It is much more highly developed than that of a human being and can be used for tracking by the direct scent of a human being or by ground scent from feet or an article. The hearing of dogs is also very acute and their ears are attuned to higher noises than the human ear is capable of hearing.

Darkness is equally no real handicap and a dog is of the greatest value to handlers in determining the presence of individuals in the vicinity who would not otherwise be revealed. A single handler accompanied by his dog can investigate a crime and make an arrest when a large number of policemen without the aid of a dog might well fail.

TRAINING

Dogs and handlers of this Force as well as from several provincial and overseas Forces are trained at the Dog Training Establishment situated in Kent, while refresher training is normally arranged within each of the four districts into which this Force (Metropolitan) is divided.

The physical side of training is constantly under review and the pattern alters and changes, as experience grows. Compulsion must be used to some extent in all exercises but there is always the risk that over repetition will become boring.

Puppies bred at the Training Establishment are, at 3 months old, allocated to handlers to be "walked" for 6 months in the division where their handlers are stationed, after which they receive a week's course in elementary obedience and nosework. When they are a year old they attend a full training course lasting from 10 to 12 weeks.

Obedience is, of course, essential in any Police dog. Indeed, dogs are not introduced to advanced functions until they are fully obedient in the general sense. Man-work exercises [Ed.: such as

* It is believed that a dog's sense of smell is about 40 times more acute than that of a human being.

tracking down a "fugitive" and nailing or attacking "criminals"],
however, are stimulating and the dog enjoys them. Elementary
agility and man-work tests are now introduced at an earlier stage of
training and it is found that a judicious mixture of obedience,
agility and man-work keeps the dog on its toes and prevents the
boredom of repetition. The aim is to get the dog to enjoy obedience
rather than to force it to be obedient. It is worth mentioning here
that dogs are no longer trained in classes but by individual tui-
tion.

Dogs are obtained from the public, preferably between the ages
of 6 and 16 months. They are, in the first instance, kept at the Dog
Training Establishment, Keston [Kent], for a period varying from
one to three weeks, in order to assess their health, physique and
working abilities. On completion of this period, if found satisfactory, they are allocated to a handler, who is given a five days course
of instruction. The dog is then taken to the home address of the
handler to begin a period of familiarization, which is most important
as it is essential to build trust and understanding between dog and
handler before serious training is undertaken.

When proficiency has been obtained in obedience, tracking, following a ground scent, the distance and age* of which is progressively increased, is introduced. Dogs are then taught to search in
open country, wooded areas, or various types of buildings for hidden criminals or property.

This is done during darkness as well as during daylight, and the
dogs are taught to give tongue when they find the suspect or articles
of property. This is particularly important, especially during the
hours of darkness. The dogs are also taught to chase and stop a
running criminal. This is done firmly and without any savaging.

It is of the greatest importance that the benefits gained during
this training course should be consolidated and developed, so dogs
and handlers attend a refresher course for one day each fortnight in
various parts of the Police District. Additionally, two consecutive
weeks are devoted annually to progressive refresher training.

It will be apparent from the foregoing that much of the success in

---

* This refers to the length of time a scent has been on the ground. The older
the scent the harder the test is for the dog.

the training and use of dogs for police purposes depends on the handlers and that the selection of the right man for the right dog—especially if the dog is a puppy—is of paramount importance. A prime consideration is that handlers must be dog lovers for, apart from using the dog for police duties, handlers are responsible for the housing, feeding, grooming and, so far as is possible, the physical fitness of their dogs. Handlers must therefore be able to show extreme tolerance toward their dogs, possess infinite patience and understanding, and be capable mentally of appreciating the known instincts of the dogs. In particular, they must be capable of studying the characteristics of their dogs and of applying those characteristics to the varied police problems which present themselves. They are also expected to show a high degree of initiative and to be good practical policemen.

Dog training and operational duty are arduous physically and handlers must therefore be physically fit and active, especially when called upon to track or chase over difficult terrain. The agility of the dogs used would serve little purpose unless the handlers were able to execute the "coup de grace" made possible by the actions of the dog.

USE OF DOGS

In London, dogs are kennelled at the homes of their handlers and normally patrol for at least seven hours a day, working early, late or night shifts. Another hour is set aside for feeding, grooming, exercising, etc.

To obtain the full value of dogs, from a deterrent as well as a detection point of view, they must be out on patrol and not kept in the background waiting for emergencies. This is particularly important where the detection of crime is concerned as time is an important factor and in order to achieve the best chance of success it is essential that dogs and handlers arrive on the scene of a crime with the minimum of delay.

The method of employing dogs must necessarily depend upon the environment of the area to be policed and varies from the urban to the rural districts; in the former the dogs patrol the vicinity of vulnerable premises and are in constant readiness in the event of emergencies; while in the rural areas they patrol from a strategic point from which they can be contacted quickly by radio.

The increased use of dog transport vehicles fitted with wireless is considerably widening the scope of use to which dogs can be put in central, urban and rural areas. The vehicles, containing 2 dogs, 2 handlers, operate on a district basis and are used for conveying dogs quickly to the scene of a crime, places where crime or rowdyism is prevalent and to distant rural areas for normal patrols on foot. It must always be remembered, however, that police dogs have been trained to work and the same dogs must not be carried in vehicles for too long a period; dogs that become soft and lazy are of no value for this work. Dogs must be kept hard and fit in order to maintain the psychological effect they have on criminals.

Impressive ceremonies attended by many notables occur in London each year when trophies are awarded outstanding dogs of the Metropolitan Police force.

The most coveted award is the Black Knight Trophy instituted by Lady Violet Munnings in 1956 in memory of her well-known Pekinese named Black Knight. It consists of a magnificent gold cup and a "Dog of the Year" rosette.

Holman was a very proud and happy man on the occasion of the first presentation even though he was worried about Rex's increasing illness. Rex III won it—politely permitting Lady Munnings to withdraw a bouquet of flowers from his mouth and "shaking hands" with her when the trophy was formally presented. The trophy in subsequent years was awarded as follows: 1957 Joe; 1958 Sabu; 1959 Fritz; 1960 Amico; 1961 Rusty 12; 1962 Peter 6 and Rex 92; 1963 Colonel; 1964 Nero.

In 1962 Mr. Vincent Routledge instituted an annual and also highly prized award known as the Routledge Trophy to be presented to Metropolitan Police dogs for outstanding performances in interdistrict competitions. No. 2 District won the first competition held in 1962 with Duke, Rex 92 and Shane 5. In

1963 No. 4 District won with Chance, Rusty 12 and Timus, and in 1964 No. 2 District won with Simon 4, Rex 92 and Mizar.

To the English, police dogs are V.I.P.s who ask for little, give much in the line of duty and should be duly honored. They have rendered eminent service and will continue to do so, by night, by day, in foul and fair weather.

As Holman said aptly in his book:

I have yet to hear of a well-trained police dog turning against its handler or failing to do its duty to the best of its ability. . . . Remember that a dog is probably the only friend you have who is prepared to die for you.

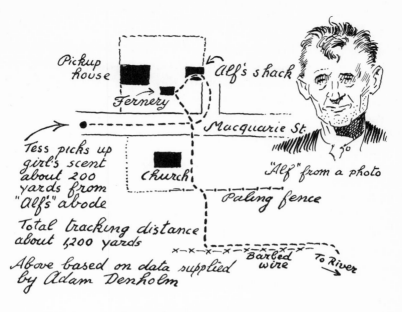

Pickup house

Fernery

Alf's shack

Macquarie St.

Tess picks up girl's scent about 200 yards from "Alf's" abode

Church

"Alf" from a photo

Paling fence

Total tracking distance about 1,200 yards

Above based on data supplied by Adam Denholm

Barbed wire

To River

I must become a borrower of the night for a dark hour or twain.

—SHAKESPEARE, *Macbeth*

9

Terror at Christmas

PIGTAILS bobbing, eyes aglow, Marcia Hayes bounded through the door of her parents' shop in Windsor, Australia, and skipped gaily toward a group of young playmates in a nearby street. The six-year-old girl left the store

at about 10 A.M. on December 24, 1937. A bright sun shone in a
cloudless sky. The air was warm and humid, a typical summer
day in the "down under" town in New South Wales, some 35
miles west of Sydney.

Marcia was a slim, pretty child, pink-cheeked with light
brown hair and dancing blue eyes, endowed with a cheerful,
friendly disposition. On this day she was neatly attired in a blue
smock with white polka dots and white starched collar, red ribbons in her hair. Marcia was barefoot, a common custom among
youngsters in smaller Australian localities during warm
weather. Laughing gaily, she swiftly joined her young friends,
unwrapping a stick of green ice covered by paper of the same
color. Her parents, Earl and Mary Hayes, were busy at the time
attending to Yuletide shoppers in their small general store.
They had given her the candy after telling her to go out to play
and to return to the store around noon.

Looking through the open doorway as Marcia tripped down
the street, one of the woman customers in the store said to Mary
Hayes; "That's a nice child you have there, a friendly little
lady."

Busy wrapping a package for the woman, an old friend
named Jessie Perry, Mary smilingly replied; "Oh, yes, Jessie, we
think she's coming along fine, and we have some nice gifts ready
for her. Of course, she has to be scolded now and then like all of
them, but she's really no trouble. Thanks for your compliment,
anyhow, and here's your package and a very Merry Christmas to
you."

"Good-bye, Jessie. Send some of your youngsters around
tonight, and they'll get some special candy," Earl said as he tied
up a package for another customer. "A very Merry Christmas to
you, and may we all have many more."

The Hayes did not give the child another thought until
lunchtime. There was no reason for any special preoccupation
on their part. They knew the youngsters she was playing with

and many adult residents of the area were friends of the family. Traffic dangers were slight and Marcia had been warned to keep to the sidewalks while playing. Windsor, a cattle-raising and agricultural center was, by any yardstick, an orderly, quiet town with a small but efficient police force.*

Shortly after noon, Marcia's parents sat down to lunch in a cheerful mood. In the center of the table was a cake with MERRY CHRISTMAS in iced letters on its chocolate covering. The minutes ticked by and both had finished their light repast of meat and salad before either was prickled by concern over Marcia. Her chair remained empty. Marcia's father finished a cup of coffee and exchanged a glance with his wife.

"I say, Mary, this is a bit odd, it's not like Marcia. We told her to return and you know she's got a good appetite," he said. "Let's take a look at the street."

His wife agreed and both left the table and proceeded to the main door and scanned the street. No children were in sight. Hurriedly the Hayes left their shop and went to the homes of some of the youngsters she had been playing with. Her friends were all under ten and were somewhat vague as to what had happened to Marcia. Yes, they had played with her and one of them had seen her strolling around a corner. It was near lunchtime and this playmate, a boy, had thought she was returning home by a somewhat roundabout way. She had not reappeared.

The parents, increasingly worried, notified local police and the men of the small force immediately instituted a search of the area where the girl had last been seen, gradually expanding the investigation to other terrain. The news of the missing child spread fast and many friends of the couple, who were well liked in the town, and others joined in the quest. Side streets, yards,

* Windsor today has a population of about 7000 but the town itself was smaller and the number of residents considerably less in 1937. It is the third oldest town in Australia. Sydney is the oldest and Parramatta, also in New South Wales, the second oldest.

gardens, fields, the banks of the nearby Hawkesbury River and various creeks were searched, the waters dragged at several points. The results were negative. The belief that the child might have met with some accident gave way to suspicions that she had been the victim of foul play.

All thoughts of Christmas Eve festivities vanished from the minds of Marcia's parents. Her father had participated actively in the search until close to dusk, which occurs at about 7 P.M. in Australia at this time of year. He was sitting in his living room trying to console his distraught wife when a friend dropped in.

"I have an idea which might help, it's just a suggestion," the man said after a quiet exchange of greetings. "Has anybody checked up on 'Old Alf,' you know him, the bloke who lives on the Pickup grounds? I know he's never done anything serious but it might be worth a little questioning."

"Oh, yes, I know Alf all right," Earl replied. "I think no one has questioned him. I've heard the police are about to stop their searching, in about an hour. I think I'll take a walk over to the Pickup place right now, it's not too far. Probably nothing will come of it but you never know and I will notify the police if something develops. They've hit a stone wall so far, it's terrible."

Alf, also known as "Goat Alf," was a well-known character in the town, a sixty-five-year-old man of small stature with a weazened, weather-beaten face whose real name was Alfred Spicer. A bachelor, who had never married as far as was known, he had been an oddball resident of the town for many years. He was employed as a gardener by a couple named Pickup, hardworking, highly respected townspeople. Alf lived in a toolshed in the rather large garden surrounding their house on the fringe of town, about ten minutes' walk from the Hayes' apartment above the store. In the shed Alf had rigged up a small kitchen-living room and slept in a tiny bedroom next to it. Near the shed was a glass-enclosed structure devoted to the care of ferns and some other plants. Although he was something of an eccentric, Spicer was a reasonably good worker, keeping the garden in tip-top condition and regularly doing odd jobs around the town, painting or repairing fences, mowing lawns and executing minor household repairs.

He had never been guilty of disorderly conduct and had not incurred the enmity of the police or other townspeople. The little money he made seemed to suffice for his needs. From time to time he got mildly drunk but during these spells he remained quietly in his toolshed home. Youngsters in the town had frequently teased him with shouts of "Goat!" as he passed by in dirty clothes, his gray hair tousled and matted. He seemed to like children, however, and showed no particular anger on these occasions. Sometimes he had chased his tormentors away with angry cackles and a raised fist but that was all. If on some occasions his opaque, close-set eyes dwelled overlong on some little girl, no one had noticed it.

Acting on the advice of his friend, who left the shop to keep a Christmas Eve social engagement, Earl told his wife he would be back shortly and headed for the Pickup home on MacQuarie Street, which was within short walking distance. At about 7 P.M. Hayes entered the Pickup home. Both Mr. and Mrs. Pickup were in the house, having returned home from work about an hour earlier. Answering Earl's queries, both expressed doubt that Alfred was in any way involved in Marcia's disappearance. They had seen him puttering in the garden when they left the house in the morning and he had told them he intended to work there all day. They said he probably was in the toolshed at that very moment and Mr. Pickup agreed to accompany Hayes across the garden to the shed to question him.

Spicer was inside and opened the door, yawning, obviously

aroused from a catnap by the knocks of his visitors. He was quite sober, dressed in blue jeans, rumpled shirt and sneakers.

"Alf, you know me, I'm Hayes, you've been in my store," Earl said. "Did you by chance at any time today see my small daughter Marcia? She was in a blue dress. She's lost, do you know about it?"

Spicer did not seem troubled by the question or the sudden arrival of the two men.

"Ah! I heard something about a search, or something, but that's none of my business," he replied. "A little girl did stop this morning, right near this door. I think she wore a blue dress, I'm not quite sure about that, I'm kind of fuzzy sometimes. Maybe she was your daughter. She said her name was Marcia and smiled. I gave her a cheerio and handed her some flowers. I just gave her some flowers, that was all. She went away down the street. No, I know nothing else. Never saw her again. Been here all day working."

Realizing that further questioning was futile at the moment, Marcia's father returned to his home and disconsolately reported the outcome of his trip to his wife. They agreed that it would be time enough to notify the police of the interrogation in the morning if they deemed it advisable.

Shortly before midnight a woman friend on her way home saw the lights lit in the Hayes' apartment and dropped in to console them. Both parents were by this time frantic with worry and she could do little to cheer them up. The police, she had learned, had stopped the search but would continue the operation early on Christmas Day. Nothing had been found; there were no clues. After some minutes of conversation, the visitor said she had to hurry home and Hayes, as a gesture of courtesy, said he would accompany her.

The woman's residence was near that of the Pickups. Their journey, on foot, would take them along MacQuarie Street. The streets of the town were deserted and quiet when the pair departed from the Hayes' house. Reaching a point close to the Pickup garden, they were startled by a noise in a nearby hedge. Then a shape appeared above the low shrubbery, apparently the shoulders and head of a man, its outline weird and barely distinguishable in the darkness.

"Hah! You've caught me at last, eh, ha, ha, hi, hi!" the apparition cackled, the man bobbing up and down in obvious excitement, the upper part of his face a pale blur in the night.

He then vanished before the startled pair could ask him a question.

"Heavens, that must be Alf," the woman said clutching Hayes' arm. "I've never heard of him acting like this before but that was his voice. I've spoken with him from time to time. And I do believe he was holding his jacket up to his ears. And what does he mean by being caught at last?"

"Oh, yes, it's Alf all right, playing some prank no doubt," Earl replied. "You know about what he told me earlier but I think I'll give the police a word about this tonight. It's no use awakening the Pickups now. They surely are sound asleep; all the lights are out."

Earl saw the woman to her door and hurried back to the center of town and reported the incident to the police officer on duty.

"Well, let's go and have a check," the sergeant on duty said and both headed for MacQuarie Street in a police car. Although it was by this time about 1 A.M. they found Alf still awake, puttering about in the shed in which a light was still on.

When the pair entered—the door was not locked—Alf cocked his head and looked inquiringly at the two men.

"What's up, what do you want?" he asked querulously.

"Oh, we're just here to look around," the sergeant said. "Do you know anything about that girl you saw this morning?"

"I told everything I know to this man here who says he's her father," Alf replied. "I just gave her some flowers, nice flowers, and I never saw her again."

"All right, Alf, all right, but I want to search this place anyhow and then that will be all for tonight, Alf," the sergeant said.

"Search if you want to," Alf replied. "There's nothing around. What have you got against me anyway? I'm just an old one. I mind my business. I ain't done any wrong, you know it."

A rather careful search of the premises yielded no clues, neither did investigation of nearby terrain by flashlight. The sergeant and Hayes decided it was unnecessary to awaken the Pickups at that hour, that they could be questioned in the morning. Dispirited and both tired and sleepy, the policeman and the child's father returned to town, the sergeant bidding good night to his companion at the door of the Hayes' home.

At dawn the search was resumed by the police and numerous townspeople. The day was again cloudless and warm. Marcia still seemed to have vanished into thin air. The police questioned the Pickups and informed them of Alf's strange behavior at the hedge. The pair said they had gone to bed before midnight and had slept soundly until breakfast time. They told the police that Alf was liable to say and do odd things, that on a number of occasions he had startled passersby with similar buffoonery. Early that morning he had informed them that he was going to another part of town to complete some repairs in a barn.

Mr. Hayes joined the searchers early in the morning, still suspicious of Alf. Scanning a section of roadway near the Pickup house, he spotted a bit of green paper half-obscured by dust lying on the ground. It was identical to the paper wrapped around the green ice Marcia had been given the previous day.

He turned the find over to the police but it was not considered very significant in view of the old man's admission that the girl had been in that area on December 24.

During the afternoon it was learned that police had contacted the Sydney constabulary for the aid of a man-dog team. At first there was some skepticism among the Windsor residents about such a move. The search had been exhaustive, scores of persons had been questioned; result nothing. Could a dog really help? When news came that Tess and Constable Adam Denholm were being sent to Windsor, everyone, including the skeptics, felt that the local police action was a wise one.

Tess, a black-coated German shephered bitch, was Australia's most famous canine detective, the Dox of down under. Denholm, nicknamed "Scotty" by his friends because of his Scottish ancestry, and his highly trained dog had performed outstandingly in numerous cases, their feats cited widely by the press and radio.

Denholm, then in his early thirties, was one of the ace police dog handlers in the world. In 1926 he had won the middleweight amateur boxing championship of Queensland and was still in fine athletic form. Tess, weighing some 80 pounds, was in her prime, a young dog with a superb tracking ability.

Scotty had just finished a delectable Christmas dinner prepared by his attractive wife in their modest Sydney home when the telephone jangled. Police headquarters, immediate departure, child missing, Windsor. Denholm, of course, stated he would report immediately with Tess, who was in the room, for the Denholms kept her on their property. Inwardly, Scotty groaned. No postprandial holiday enjoyment for him this Christmas.

At about 5 P.M., December 25, Denholm, in uniform, and Tess arrived in Windsor. The handler was not very happy about the time lapse—almost 30 hours after Marcia's disappearance. After a brief conference with local police, the team went into action.

Tess was led to the Hayes' home after Denholm made her smell the piece of green paper that had contained the ice. At the child's home the bitch smelled a frock which Marcia had worn recently, a pair of shoes and socks and the child's bed.

Then Scotty and the dog proceeded to the street where the child had been playing. Tess sniffed around and found a scent, although the area had been crisscrossed by many persons and vehicles.

Held on a long tracking leash by Denholm, Tess, having obviously captured a good scent, headed away from the spot. Marcia's father and local police followed closely on the heels of the man-dog team. Crowds of curious onlookers had been ordered to remain at a distance so as not to confuse the animal in its quest.

Hardly wavering in her course, the Alsatian led Denholm and some local policemen to Alf's shed. The old man was not on the premises when the policemen and Tess entered the structure. Denholm had been informed that he probably would not be present in view of what he had told the Pickups that morning.

Inside the house, the dog sniffed around the living room and then entered the small bedroom. Here she smelled everywhere and then suddenly, as if coming to some kind of decision, jumped upon the bed and began to paw vigorously at the shabby blankets on it. A few seconds of this activity seemed to satisfy her. She jumped off the bed and quietly sat down on the floor, eyes flicking at Scotty and seeming to say, "My job is done for today."

The policemen gave the bed a thorough combing but nothing incriminating was visible.

Puzzled, the local police sergeant in command looked questioningly at Denholm.

"I believe Tess's actions indicate that for her this is the end of the trail," Denholm said. "She thinks the child was on that bed and I am quite sure she is right. I also believe this—that my dog senses that the child did not leave the bed alive."

"Possibly so, but the body must be somewhere," the sergeant replied.

Denholm looked around the room and spotted a shirt hanging on a nail high on one wall.

"Let's give Tess a good sniff at that shirt. I think she missed it in her first try," Denholm said. "It may give her some new ideas."

He took down the shirt and the dog smelled it intensely. This seemed to convey something to the dog and she was off again, still on the long leash, her nostrils probing the ground. She led the police and Hayes out of the house and into the garden. Here Tess headed straight for the fernery.

"By Jove! I never knew there was a fernery around here," the sergeant exclaimed. "I failed to take a look at that when I surveyed the garden with Earl early this morning."

Tess flicked her nose here and there in the fernery and in a spot where plants were particularly dense she pawed the ground and whined. But there was nothing there or elsewhere in the structure of interest to the police. Tess, apparently satisfied that this search sufficed, then led the men out of the garden, across MacQuarie Street and through a churchyard. She was clearly on some hot scent, and pulled relentlessly at her leash, forcing the men into a run. Emerging from the churchyard, she leaped easily over a six-foot-high paling fence and was halted momentarily as Denholm, leash in hand, and the others clambered over it. Heading into the paddocks (meadows) she continued her rapid pace, keeping the leash at maximum tautness.

Gradually, Denholm and the dog pulled ahead of the others, so steady was Tess's pace and thrust. At one point she stopped alongside a barbed-wire fence and sniffed excitedly, pawing the ground and whining. This only lasted a few seconds and she moved onward, more or less following her original direction.

She did not halt until she reached the willow-bordered banks of a 40-foot-wide creek, a tributary of the Hawkesbury River, about 1,200 yards from the Pickup grounds. This area had been thoroughly searched and the water dragged for a considerable distance during the daylight hours of the preceding day but nothing had been found. There was nothing worth finding in the water at that time, as was later disclosed.

Tess had tracked so furiously that even Denholm, a good runner, was puffing hard when he and his dog reached the bank. The other searchers at this moment were some distance behind, but coming up as fast as they could.

Sniffing the ground and the air, the dog gave a sudden lunge and the leash slipped out of Denholm's hand. She then plunged into the water and started swimming through the reeds and bulrushes which fringed the bank. Following her, but halting at the water's edge, Denholm saw Tess threshing around a brown sack floating in the water, trying hard to obtain a firm hold on it with her teeth. At this hour, shortly after 6 P.M., shadows were-lengthening but visibility was still good, since darkness comes in Australia in December at 7:30 P.M. The bag obviously was a common potato sack and apparently contained something weighty.

"Get it, Tess, bring it in!" Denholm shouted encouragingly.

When the policemen and the father came hurrying up they were as excited as Denholm over the dog's find.

"Damnation, Scotty, get that bag quick, your dog is having trouble with it," one of the policemen shouted.

The father at this moment let out a gasp and, fully clothed, plunged into the stream, whose depth ranged from five to nine feet. Half-wading, half-swimming, he made his way to the sack and the dog. Tess let out one whine but that was all when he grasped the bag with his arms below water and pulled it ashore.

Tess followed him up the bank, shook herself thoroughly and

dutifully returned to Denholm's side, tail wagging, the wet leash slithering behind her. As Hayes handed the dripping bag to one of the policemen it broke open, having been loosely tied. The lower part of two small legs slipped into view. As Hayes broke into sobs, the policeman laid his burden on the ground and removed the body of a young girl. She was dead. It was Marcia—still in her blue polka-dot dress, red ribbons in her dripping hair.

At the sight of the body the father shouted in anguish, "Just give me two minutes with that old bastard, he did it, I'll finish him off with these two hands!"

He started running away but was pursued and calmed by the police, who assured him that the murderer would be made to pay for his crime via the law.

Examining the bag, Denholm and the other policemen noted that no lead or stone weights had been placed in it and that it bore stains of green paint.

In accordance with Australian police procedure, one of the officers left the scene and soon returned with the police medical examiner in an ambulance which they parked on a nearby country road. The examiner pronounced the girl dead and expressed the conviction she had been strangled, possibly raped. The body was then transported to the ambulance and the vehicle bore the men and the dog back to town.

When the father broke the tragic news to his wife she collapsed and was given sedation by a doctor. While excited crowds milled in the streets the police succeeded without great delay in rounding up the aged gardener.

Taken to police headquarters, Spicer at first stuck to his story that he had not seen the child since he had given her some flowers on the morning of the 24th.

"What about that green paint on one of your ears?" a flint-eyed constable asked.

"Oh, that! I was painting a fence with green paint recently,"

Spicer said. "I must have touched my ear with the brush; yes, that's it."

The interrogator whipped the potato sack which he had been holding behind his back around his body and shook it in front of Alf's eyes.

"It so happens, Alf, that the green on your ear is just the same color as the paint on this bag, this wet bag which Marcia was in—she was murdered, you know," the policeman shouted.

"Er, yes, I think I stood my paintpot on the bag, y-y-yes-s, I think that was it," Alf replied, his jaws working.

"Do you swear you just saw her once yesterday, that you gave her flowers, nothing else?" the policeman exclaimed threateningly.

It was all over in a few minutes of questioning, Alf sobbing out:

"I get funny feelings many times, crazy feelings. Leave me alone, leave me alone! I gave her the flowers and she went away saying she would come back again after she brought the flowers home. She came back . . . and I found that she was dead."

Further questioning after formal arrest revealed that Alf had lured Marcia into his abode about noontime on the 24th. Once inside, he seized her and raped her on the bed. She screamed and he strangled her on the bed. There was no one in the immediate vicinity of the shed. He stuffed the body of Marcia, with her dress on, into the bag and dumped it and its contents in a corner of the fernery where leafage was profuse. He then returned to the shed, somewhat hazily formulating plans to hide the body elsewhere after nightfall.

Shortly before 11 P.M. on the 24th Alf returned to the fernery, tied up the bag, and headed for the creek via the churchyard and the paddocks. No one spied him. Being fairly agile in spite of his age, he scrambled over the six-foot-high paling without particular difficulty, the bag on his shoulder. Reaching the creek he stood on the bank and flung the bag containing the body into the bulrushes and then returned to his shed by another route.

It was on his return from this grisly journey that he beheld Hayes and the woman he was escorting. He believed in his twisted brain that his crime had been discovered and this prompted him to cackle, "Caught at last!" He realized after hiding in some other shrubbery that there was no particular significance to this encounter and returned to the shed.

When Hayes and the Pickups questioned Alf early in the evening of December 24 the body of the girl was in the fernery. The corpse was no longer there, however, when Hayes and the policemen searched the shed and its vicinity in the early morning of Christmas Day. The sack was not in the water when the creek area was searched and dragged on the 24th.

Tess had been uncannily right in her reaction after sniffing the bed. Death had come there. Alf had placed Marcia in the bag while she lay on the bed and then had carried her body to the fernery. The scent of the girl as a result had practically vanished in the room as far as Tess's nose was concerned. The dog became particularly excited in the fernery and at the barbed-wire fence because at these two points she apparently again got good whiffs of the girl's scent. Spicer had momentarily placed the bag on the ground at the barbed-wire fence to decide just what direction he should take from there. Tess probably could have picked up his trail back to the shed but discovery of the body and the fact that the trail had led to the creek from the shed had virtually convinced Denholm that Spicer was the culprit. Further tracking was not deemed necessary.

A full medical report confirmed that Marcia had been raped and strangled. She had been wearing a pair of panties under her dress when she left the store in the morning but this apparel was never found. Alf could not recall where he had hidden the panties and a major search for this item was not deemed necessary in view of the solution of the murder.

If the murderer had been a more intelligent man and had suitably weighted the bag with stones or chunks of lead, the man-dog hunt might have taken longer. It is doubtful whether it would have failed completely, however. Tess was on a definite track and her actions from the very start of the quest indicated that Spicer was implicated. If weighted, the bag certainly would not have been visible but a further dragging of the creek at that point would have revealed it.

The accomplishment of Tess was rather unique, a case of "double tracking." She led police to the site of the murder correctly, then picked up the trail of the murderer which resulted in the finding of the body. As a result of this activity Alf was doomed. The whole operation was something of a record in crime solution as regards elapsed time. The body had been found in about one hour's time after the team had gone into action.

Scotty, now an inspector in the Sydney force, has personally aided this author with many details of the case via letter. In one letter he provided the following additional information regarding the discovery of the body.

"The corpse," he wrote, "had been thrown into the creek apparently from the bank and had lodged in a clump of bulrushes. These were protruding from the water. Some were under the bag, suspending it and preventing it from going to the bottom. The bulrushes anchored the bag and prevented it from drifting away with the current. A body will sink if dropped into water shortly after death but as body gases start to generate in a body it tends to float. I am of the opinion that in this case the bulrushes were supporting the bag. It was close to high tide when we came on the scene and only a few inches of the bag were above water. At low tide more of it would have been visible."

The speed with which the case was solved with the aid of the dog was of great importance. Probably the bag would have been spotted ultimately by someone, even if it had drifted. But more days, even weeks, might have elapsed before this discovery. This might have given Alf the opportunity of suddenly disappearing from the town. Or he could have returned to the creek at night after all official searching had ended and, removing the body, buried it deep in some lonely spot. With the body lying undiscovered underground it would have been very difficult to put the finger on him since there were no witnesses of his meeting with the girl and her entry into his shed.

What prompted Marcia to wander toward the Pickup grounds instead of returning home will never be known. Spicer stubbornly stuck to his story that she had suddenly appeared before his shed in the morning and that he had then lured her inside.

Tess and Scotty returned to Sydney that Christmas night, her handler a very proud man. At home there was tasty refreshment for the constable as he discussed details of the tragic case with his wife and some friends. There also were some gastronomic treats for Tess.

The next day the story was splashed in the press. Many reporters and photographers visited Denholm either at his home or at his police station to obtain information and take photographs of him and his dog. The hubbub when reporters came to the Denholm house did not greatly distract Tess in her very personal task—doting on a cluster of puppies she had brought into the world earlier that month.

Denholm was present at the trial of Spicer. At one point the defense questioned whether the fact that a dog had pursued various scents could be regarded as any type of valid evidence in such a case. The objection was not sustained. The jury retired for less than an hour before returning a verdict of guilty. Alf was hanged.

Tess died from natural causes during World War II years. Before her death she and her master had handled many other cases with credit. During recent years the use of police dogs in fighting crime virtually ended in Australia, largely due to the difficulties of breeding the right dogs and the expense involved in canine importation from distant countries.

Scotty Denholm now lives with his wife in Castlecrag, Sydney. He has two sons. One is twenty-eight years old and is in the bus transportation business and the other, twenty years old, is a police constable stationed at North Sydney. Denholm's wife has been active for many years posing as a matron model for fashion photographers and also is regularly featured in TV commercials.

In a letter sent to me early last year (1966) Scotty said he planned to retire as an Inspector of the Sydney police when he attained his sixtieth birthday on October 5, 1966. In retirement he planned to write a book about dogs to be entitled *My Canine Cobbers.* (Cobber is Australian slang for friend, pal, mate.)

"Did you know," he wrote in the same letter, "that when Tess died the authorities had a taxidermist preserve her (he made a terrible job of her too) and she was on view at the Sydney Museum for years. Last year they donated her back to the Police Department and she is now housed in the Office of the Police Training Center Stables. But she does not look anything like the dog I knew and, yes, loved. Many people boasted that they had a pup from Tess but when asked to quote her pedigree, they never could inform me of Tess's correct name, which was Olympic Bonanza. Tess was only her kennel name. She was a fine cobber to me to the very last."

In Conclusion

GUNS cracked in the hills of central Pennsylvania as the final pages of this book were written and William Holenbaugh, ex-convict, kidnapper, madman, came to a bloody end in one of the biggest manhunts in this country's history.

Alsatian police dogs were among the hunters. Two of them were killed and one wounded when the elusive "Mountain Man" blasted away at policemen and dogs closing in on his shack at Shade Gap. FBI agent Terry Anderson also was mortally wounded. The end came for Holenbaugh the following day; the girl he had kidnapped was miraculously rescued unharmed.

This was one of those cases in which dogs did not prove useful, as often happens in K-9 action along with the many successful missions. At the spot where Holenbaugh had seized Peggy Bradnick the footsteps of the man and the girl vanished in rocky ground a few hundred yards distant. The dogs, all trained man trackers, were led to the scene by police but could not find any useful scent trail after giving the ground a nosing. Perhaps they arrived too late on the spot, possibly the area had been criss-crossed too often by various people. The six Bradnick children, who had descended from a school bus, were standing on a highway when the abductor, wearing high rubber boots, made off with Mary. The children were regularly picked up and deposited at this point by bus during school days, leaving or returning to their home by a dirt road branching off from the highway. Aside from possible negating weather conditions, the factor of confusing scents undoubtedly was present when the dogs got there. Not being an experienced police dog handler, I do not wish the reader to draw any particular conclusions from these facts but they are worth noting as far as K-9 operations are concerned. Perhaps even such champions as Dox, Rex III and Tess might have come away baffled.

Let it be said to the honor of the dogs that all were good coppers who obeyed orders and did their best in the finest tradition of canine law enforcers.

One very important aspect of dog law enforcement, although not strictly a police undertaking, has been mentioned only briefly in this book and deserves a few more words. This is the use of dogs as guards in big department stores.

The world's largest department store, Macy's Herald Square, in the heart of New York City, is a pioneer in this type of special security in the United States. The store installed canine guards on October 17, 1952. All the dogs are Doberman pinschers as carefully trained and used as any police dogs.

The principal aim of the dog corps was to curb heavy losses inflicted by "sleep-ins" or after-hour pilferers—thieves who enter a store before closing and remain overnight to vanish in the morning with their loot.

At Macy's, guards take one or more dogs on regular patrols through the store on leash at night. The results from the very initiation of the project have been highly satisfactory, and the technique has been adopted by many stores other than Macy's.

Traumatic experiences have befallen those nimble-fingered

gentry brave enough or stupid enough to try their hand at this type of night thievery. To any smart thief, the 2,000,000-square-foot Macy "empire" should be permanently off limits. The mere sight of a Doberman, whose appearance is somehow more sinister than that of an Alsatian or almost any other dog, with its jaws open, snarling, ready to attack, is the stuff of which very bad dreams are made. When these canine noses are sniffing around in either light or dark places in a store, capture of a thief is virtually a foregone conclusion. Fortunately, no "sleep-in" has been physically hurt by the dogs in the many years of this K-9 operation, a credit to the whole *modus operandi*.

Macy's has five dogs on call at present, males and females. They are Pam, Thrifty, Flash, Suzy and Champion, their names linked in one way or another with items sold in the store. They are comfortably housed in kennels on one of the roofs. Each kennel is inside a grilled area, or cage, which provides each dog with fairly spacious exercise or walking ground.

A member of the security department showed me around not long ago on what proved to be a very interesting morning. Except for one or two barks, the dogs watched us with aloof alertness when we arrived in the kennel area.

Complementing the work of men and dogs is an intricate and impressive security system, one of the most modern in the world: TV sets of various types, whereby a constant watch can be maintained on doorways and other key areas from a central control room; scores of portable walkie-talkies of the latest type, which permit lightning-quick communication between guards or other employees throughout the area; a special computing machine, which can almost immediately inform a suspicious employee that a person's credit card is valid or that the signature on a check is that of a person whose previous dealings with the store were not savory.

Throughout the store there is also an electronic alarm system, soundless, invisible, but mighty effective. It can be turned on whenever needed. Anyone entering this active electronic field disturbs it and thus immediately triggers an alarm.

It was explained that in spite of all this mechanized network, the dogs are very useful in more ways than trailing pilferers. They are very good at detecting smoke, water leaks, and more. On one occasion a computer was running at night when it should have been off. One of the dogs on patrol somehow realized that this was irregular and went up to it and gave tongue, after which it was turned off.

Humorous sidelights crop up. A thief decided to "stay over" after hours last year and got busy. Probably he was ignorant of the canine employees or felt they presented no danger. Two of the dogs with their handler—both animals on leash—found him hiding behind a counter and the dogs gave him a first-class dose of snarls, bared fangs and glittering eyes. He surrendered quietly. He was wearing an expensive brand-new overcoat, fresh from the men's clothing division. Haled to night court, he insisted before the judge that he had been attacked by five—yes, five—ferocious dogs and that their guard in a threatening manner had forced him to put on the overcoat so that he could prove theft was involved. Since he was uninjured and his story obviously fishy, the presiding judge suggested that it might be helpful to have the particular dogs brought into court to establish just how many were involved.

This was too much for the thief. "No, sir, please don't bring those dogs in here," he mumbled. "I was stealing, but I don't want to see those dogs again, never."

Macy's has other stores in the New York area, and the canine guards from Manhattan and their handlers can be sped to these buildings by car if called for.

In conclusion, the attention of dog owners should be drawn to an important warning emanating from a very authoritative source, the American Kennel Club. It is contained in an article by Arthur Frederick Jones in the magazine *Pure-Bred Dogs*

American Kennel Gazette of February, 1953, entitled "Police Dog Training Is Not for Our Pets."

After stressing the fact that due to various world conditions there is more crime in every community today than has been known before in modern times, the writer counsels that only trained handlers should have dogs designed for a serious purpose, such as law enforcement.

In the November issue [November, 1952] we spoke of these conditions and suggested that one of the answers was the use by police departments of trained dogs in charge of trained men. That is still our suggestion and one that can be made to work in American communities, just as it has proved successful in many European towns and cities. However, this suggestion should not be confused with anything else. Police-trained dogs can do a grand job under proper training and control but—most decidedly—they are not suited to private ownership in the capacity of pets.

No one would think of letting a child play with a high-powered car with the motor running for, despite its wonderful engineering and great utility, such an automobile can be an instrument of destruction in the hands of a youngster. Yet many novices, today, seem to be overlooking something that can be just as destructive in the hands of the untutored—the dog that is trained for police or army duty.

In recent weeks the American Kennel Club has had countless requests for the names of trainers who can take dogs and give them police and guard training. In every instance there has been made an effort to explain to these people that they would be playing with dynamite. And no names of trainers have been supplied to anyone who wanted such a trained dog to keep about the house. However, some of the people were so insistent that there remains a feeling that they will keep trying other sources of information.

The fact is that the average citizen does not need a trained dog. Any dog can be a guard. Size is not a real consideration. In fact, some of the toy breeds are even more alert than the big fellows. A housebreaker, hearing a dog bark, does not stop to figure out the size of the dog. Most times he gets out of the vicinity as fast as he can, for the whole success of his illegal venture depends on silence. To be sure, we've all heard of robberies made possible because the burglars knew how to fraternize with dogs, but those are such unusual cases that they make big headlines every time. And in most instances there were other factors that entered into the situation.

The average dog barks because he is startled and frightened. That's one reason why the little fellows do such a wonderful job. They're more easily startled, particularly at night. But fright is not the only measure of a dog's value. All dogs have a sense of responsibility, and they practically all sound off at strangers.

So let's content ourselves with owning dogs of those breeds that appeal to us the most and leave highly specialized forms of training to the specialists who know what they are doing. Let's not risk having our children and friends injured merely because they do not know how to act around dogs that really have no place in the average home. Let's not think of the dog as a cure-all in himself.

Wise counsel for any dog owner and one which experts like Maimone, Holman, Denholm, Steinberg, Richardson and so many others no doubt would roundly endorse.

A major role in the development of outstanding German shepherd dogs in this country has been undertaken by the Fidelco Breeders Foundation, Inc., a nonprofit organization, its headquarters in Bloomfield, Connecticut. The primary aim of the organization is "to produce German Shepherd dogs that will possess the fundamental qualities that will make them fit and capable of service as guide dogs for the blind and to work with law enforcement and security agencies, government and private."

Fidelco has furnished many excellent Alsatians to police K-9 departments in this country, including two dogs of the Freeport police. Its staff is engaged in very vital scientific research in regard to hip dysplasia, an abnormal development of the hip joint, highly prevalent in nearly all purebred breeds, particularly the large breeds like the Alsatians. The organization is succeeding in eradicating this weakness in its dogs through intensive research and careful breeding. Persons interested in this program can obtain an exceptionally fine booklet from Fidelco defining its purpose, procedures and aspirations. The booklet also contains numerous absorbing stories about Fidelco dogs in police and other work.

Readers of this book desiring further information on the London police dog training methods will find valuable advice in a comprehensive manual entitled *Police Dogs—Training and Care*. It can be obtained from Her Majesty's Stationery Office, York House, Kingsway, London, W.C. 2, England (price ten shillings). Its contents are fully approved by British police officials.

Bibliography

A Partial List of Sources

Barbaresi, Sara, *How to Raise and Train a German Shepherd*. New York, Sterling, 1957.

Berdez, A., *Anleitung zur Dressur und Verwendung für den Polizei und Kriegshund*. Germany, Wyss Publishing Co., 1913.

"Bloodhound—Most Misunderstood Dog." *Science Digest* (November, 1951).

Bonuzzi, Guglielmo, *Gli animali si vogliono bene*. Rome, Cappelli Publishing Co., 1964.

"Canine Cops." *Reader's Digest* (December, 1936).

Chapman, Samuel G., *Dogs in Police Work*. Chicago, Public Administration Service, 1960.

"The Dog as a Guard," in *Modern Dog Encyclopedia*. Harrisburg and New York, Stackpole and Heck, 1949.

Forster, E. S., *Dogs in Ancient Warfare*. New York, Oxford University Press, 1941.

Furnas, J. C., "Four Footed Cops." *Saturday Evening Post* (September 22, 1956).

Holman, Arthur, *My Dog Rex*. New York, Funk, 1958.

Koenig, Kurt, *Mein Freund Hussan*. Giessen, Germany, Bruhlischer Verlag, 1958.

Lo Bello, Nino, "Dox, the Super Sleuth." *Argosy Magazine* (August, 1965).

Loxton, Howard, *Dogs, Dogs, Dogs*. London, Paul Hamlyn, Ltd., 1962.

Marders, Irvin E., *How to Use Dogs Effectively in Modern Police Work*. Police Science Press, 1960.

Military Dog Training and Employment. Washington Headquarters, Department of the Army (USA), 1960.

Monahan, J., "Ben Gets His Man." *Reader's Digest* (March, 1952).

Richardson, Edwin, *My Forty Years with Dogs*. London, Hutchinson & Co., 1925.

———, *War, Police and Watch Dogs*. London, Blackwood, 1910.

"Royal Canadian Mounted Police Service Dogs," an illustrated brochure reprinted from *The RCMP Quarterly* (October, 1960).

Schmidt, Friedo, *Polizeihund*. Augsburg, Germany, P. J. Pfeiffer, 1911.

Trapman, A. H., *Man's Best Friend*. New York, Macaulay Publishing Co., 1928.

Note: Much of the vast literature on dogs and their activities in anticrime work and other fields is available to students in the reference division of the New York Public Library at 42d Street and Fifth Avenue. See "Dogs" in index drawers for this material.

Index

Index

American Kennel Club, 224, 225, 226
Athens, 41
Avalanche dogs, 38

Ben, London's Labrador, 33, 160, 161, 183–186
Binks, 68–73
Blackmail, 87
Bloodhounds, history of, 83–88
Bonuzzi, Guglielmo, 59, 125

Canadian dogs, 109, 110
Casper, 17–37
Chips, 33
Corinth, 45
Cupparas, 41, 42

De Martino, Carmine, 141, 142
Denholm, Adam, 211, 220
Denmark, 111, 112
Dixon, Edward, 19, 20, 21
Doberman, 32
Donges, Norman, 120, 123
Dox, 114–150

Epirus, 40, 41
Ethiopians, 46

Fidelco, 226, 227
Freeport, L.I., 17–36

Gelert, 58
German shepherd breeding, 31, 32
Germany, operations in, 102, 108, 109
Ghent, 36, 100, 101
Giuliano, Salvatore, 129–133

Hamid, Sultan, 93
Hayes, Marcia, 203, 220
Henry of Valois, 52
Hercules, 52, 53
Holman, Arthur, 152–183

Jarl, 36

Koenig, Kurt, 64

London police, 187–201

Mack the Knife, 106
Macy's, 32, 222–224
Maimone, Giovanni, 24, 35, 114–150
Menconi, Valeria, 142–144
Mons, 48
Montdidier, Aubry de, 53–57

New York City dogs, 95–97

Oslo, 36

Pyrrhus, 40, 41

Remote control dogs, 38
Rex, 152–183

Spicer, Alfred, 206, 220
Steinberg, Gary, 17–37
Solferino, 74, 75
Stephanitz, Max von, 102

Trapman, A. H., 61–64

U.S. Army manual, 59–61

William of Orange, 49, 50, 51